AL & RON LINDNER

Reflections at
First
Light

HARVEST HOUSE PUBLISHERS
EUGENE, OREGON

Cover by Left Coast Design, Portland, Oregon

Cover and interior photos © Bill Lindner Photography

REFLECTIONS AT FIRST LIGHT
Copyright © 2015 Al Lindner and Ron Lindner
Published by Harvest House Publishers
Eugene, Oregon 97402
www.harvesthousepublishers.com

ISBN 978-0-7369-6425-8 (pbk.)
ISBN 978-0-7369-6426-5 (eBook)

Printed in the United States of America

15 16 17 18 19 20 21 22 23 / VP-CD / 10 9 8 7 6 5 4 3 2 1

Contents

Introduction

AL LINDNER

I CAN'T REMEMBER A TIME WHEN I DIDN'T fish. My earliest recollections are of summers I stayed with my grandmother on a lake near Hayward, Wisconsin. I spent countless hours fishing from the shore, wading, and occasionally fishing with my uncles in a boat. I also fished with my older brother, Ron, who is ten years my senior. If I dug the worms, seined the minnows, fixed the tackle, and loaded the boat, he would take me out with him. He told me everyone starts out as a "worm boy" apprentice, and for years I believed him.

When I was 16 and enjoying one of my many summers at my grandmother's, I entered a one-day musky derby—and won! I actually got paid for fishing. I was also interviewed by the local paper and did a snippet for the television sports news in nearby Duluth. With that incredible experience, my fate was sealed. I was destined to become a professional sport fisherman.

Growing up in Chicago, I was a mediocre student. If I had to write a book report or give a speech, my subject was fishing—always. I had no other hobbies or interests. I didn't hunt, golf, or collect stamps. In my high school yearbook, I stated that my life goal was to catch a record fish. Outside of a few jobs, the only work I've ever known has been directly related to sport fishing.

Even when an army stint took me to Vietnam, where some guys carried the New Testament with them in the field, I carried Buck Perry's *Spoonplugging* or Bill Binkelman's *Nightcrawler Secrets.* These tattered, marked, and underlined booklets were as well annotated as many of my fellow soldiers' Bibles. I could even quote many of the passages verbatim. Except for one horrible night in Vietnam when I didn't know if I would see the light of day, I gave little thought to

God or any lesser subjects that required introspection and study.*

When I returned home from Vietnam, my piscatory ambitions were running high. In 1967 Ron and I moved from Chicago to Wisconsin to Minnesota to pursue our dream of setting up a resort and guide service and restarting our small tackle-making business. From that point in my life until I retired from fishing the Bassmaster Professional Tournament circuit in 1979, I sometimes logged as many as 300 days on the water in a single year. During these halcyon years, I also promoted lures, made films for television, did radio shows, wrote magazine articles with Ron, and appeared at a seemingly endless parade of sport shows and seminars.

In retrospect, I see that the schedule was impossible to maintain for very long. Sooner or later, something had to give. Nevertheless, this apprenticeship period allowed me to explore all types of waters in every part of the country, and I kept discovering new ways to catch more and different types of fish. I learned the art and honed the skills of

---

* See chapter 1.

intuitive fishing that would serve me well in the higher ranks of my profession.

What little time I had for reading during these years was given to books such as *Man Against Musky*, the Herter's catalog, *Lucas on Bass Fishing*, and the *Fishing News*. My days were spent on the water fishing and guiding, and I devoted my nights to talking fishing in the bars. Unlike Ron, I drank mostly socially, and alcohol never became a significant problem. My real addiction was fishing, and I was hooked bigtime! I figured, why waste a day doing something else when I could be on the water—rain or shine, hot or cold, windy or calm? My occasional diversion was chasing women on the really bad-weather days.

"Some go to church and think about fishing;
others go fishing and think about God."

TONY BLAKE

All this time, the God I didn't know or care about not only allowed me to have these experiences but also kept me safe. God had a plan for my life that would turn my all-consuming passion into a lifestyle that was both acceptable and useful to Him. Not surprisingly, a few changes were in order—changes that dramatically impacted my "fish all the time" obsession.

The changes seemed to happen fast, all in the span of a few years. First I got married. Then Ron and I began publishing a magazine and producing a television show. Soon our family grew to four, and then, most importantly, I came to faith in Jesus Christ and was, as they say, born again. That changed everything.

When I received Jesus as Lord of my life, I was relieved that He did not ask me to go into some other endeavor. I was in my late thirties, and fishing was the only thing I knew how to do. He graciously allowed me to continue to fish hard in the coming decades, but He made certain that the intensity of my earlier years gave way to a more balanced mode of living. I gave up the Bassmaster and Bass Casters Association professional tournament fishing circuits, where I dearly loved to compete, and I learned to be content with a few select competitive events every year just to keep my hand in.

During this phase of life, I started attending church regularly, and with my eyes newly opened, I devoured the Bible as I once did books on fishing. I was thrilled to learn that many of Jesus's first inductees (the apostles) were fishermen and that Jesus was evidently well acquainted with life in the boat. It quickly became evident that fishing, much like farming, football, flying, or any other human endeavor, is an effective setting for modern-day parables, teeming with life lessons.

As I started to share my Christian faith with others, most of whom were fellow fishermen, I found myself naturally using fishing experiences to illustrate and explain the workings of the kingdom of God. I sensed that God, the supreme conservationist, did not intend to waste all of my earlier efforts and experiences. Instead, God used for His own purposes the gift He had given me for fishing and the fishing experiences Ron and I accumulated through our many years as professional anglers.

When Ron speaks to other fishermen about how Jesus Christ saved him from a life of alcoholism, he sometimes mentions being "scooped up by the gentle net of God's grace." He might also say, "God does not practice catch and

release. Instead, He puts us in His live well of eternal life—forever!" The patterns of our lives and our personalities are quite different, but Ron and I have found ourselves constantly sharing our faith through fishing analogies.

In this book, we retell some real-life events and experiences God has used to illuminate our lives with an understanding that He is alive, He's concerned for our good, and He's at work in the world today. He has shown Himself to Ron and me in the most routine events in our lives as well as in moments of trauma, danger, heartache, and highly charged adventure. God has shown us that we never need to walk in the darkness of where we have been, but we can live in the sweet, clear light of life in Jesus Christ.

*Come to Me, all you who labor and are
heavy laden, and I will give you rest.*

MATTHEW 11:28

Chapter One

There Are No
Atheists in Foxholes

AL LINDNER

THE SAYING "THERE ARE NO ATHEISTS IN FOX-
HOLES" is attributed to US Military Chaplain William
Thomas Cummings in a field sermon during the battle of
Bataan in 1942. President Dwight D. Eisenhower quoted
it in 1954 from the White House as part of an American
Legion program.

I grew up in Chicago in a nominal Christian household
and attended parochial schools. Yet my view of life—let alone
my prayer life—was like that of what the eighteenth-century
English cleric John Wesley termed a "sprinkled heathen."

Yes, I believed in God. How else could all the beauty of this natural world come to be? But I really didn't *believe* Him. I didn't know what His Word said or what He wanted from me or from humankind. I believed what my family, my school, and my friends believed—that Jesus was somehow God. So technically, I wasn't an agnostic or an atheist, but that is about as far as anything spiritual went.

My entire focus was on fishing, fishing, and more fishing. When the weather was extremely bad, my interest sometimes turned to girls, sometimes to social drinking, and occasionally to not-so-social drinking. I never dreamed of being a surgeon, a lawyer, an actor, or a musician.

After high school I moved to a lake cabin our family owned near Hayward, Wisconsin, to keep my widowed grandmother company, provide her with transportation, and take care of any chores that required some muscle. For work I painted houses and guided fishing parties, and I spent my evenings at the local pub, usually talking about fishing.

At this stage in life, I occasionally recited the Lord's Prayer in school or at family gatherings along with everyone else. That was the extent of my prayer life. My entire focus continued to be on fishing.

This "live to fish" attitude was interrupted in 1965. The United States military was drafting able-bodied young men and sending them to Vietnam. I thought, *If I have to go, let's get it over with*, and I pushed my draft number up.

Before I had to leave, I spent every spare moment fishing. During this six-month waiting period, I learned a lot about what would become my career and complete lifestyle. This was also when I entered the musky derby and won the $80 first-place prize—the equivalent of a week's wages in that day. This made a big impression on me and would one day motivate me as a professional tournament fisherman.

When my accelerated draft number came up, I was sent

for training to Fort Knox, Kentucky; then to Fort Gordon, Georgia; and finally to Fort Sill, Oklahoma. After this, I was bound for Vietnam, where things were really heating up. In 1966, at age 19, I found myself smack-dab on the demilitarized zone between South Vietnam and communist-controlled North Vietnam—a total hotspot—and this is where I would say the first meaningful prayer of my entire life.

I had just arrived in the country and was settling in when we came under a severe mortar attack. At the first blast, I heard that gut-wrenching warning call, *"Incoming!"* With mortar rounds raining down and slamming the entire area, I dove into the first half-built bunker I saw. Inside was a marine, and amid the explosions and utter chaos, he began screaming and cursing God at the top of his lungs. Looking skyward with clenched fists, as the mortar attack continued, he roared, "You #@*9%$# &%^#@, #*!*, #*!*#…Why are You letting this happen!" Fear surging in my stomach, my heart thumping as acid shot into my throat, I turned my head upward and somehow found myself screaming above the mayhem that was erupting around me, "I ain't with him, Lord! That ain't me talking! I've got nothin' to do with this guy!" Interesting—without thinking, I was calling Him Lord.

I later learned the marine had been up on the line for a long time and was suffering from combat neurosis, exhaustion, and post-traumatic stress disorder.

This prayer was my first real attempt at communication with the God I didn't personally know and didn't understand. That mortar attack eventually ended, but I continued to see lives stolen away much too early as casualties of war. Even so, 16 more years would pass before I called out to the Lord Jesus again under much different circumstances. In that interim, I never realized that the God I didn't believe in was directing my path and protecting me.

Al Lindner

God used prayer—which I didn't know about and didn't care to practice—to bring about one of the most refining moments in my life. Fast-forward 16 years after the foxhole prayer in Vietnam. By this time, plenty of life experiences were behind me. My brother Ron, his wife, Dolores, and my wife, Mary, had all dedicated their lives to the Lord, and I was the single holdout. Our kids were attending a private Christian school, and I often attended functions where the gospel message was proclaimed loud and clear. God was priming me. Members of my television audience began sending me fan mail and including gospel tracts. I started reconnecting with old carousing buddies whose lives had been completely transformed. Amazing changes were happening all around me. Clearly, somebody was trying to get my attention.

Mary would say nighttime prayers with our sons, but I was always a silent bystander. One night my four-year-old son asked me if I would pray. I answered, "Dad always prays alone after you guys finish." Of course, this was utterly untrue. I didn't know how to pray and didn't have the heart to pray, but I was too ashamed to say so.

Later that night, when everyone else was in bed, I passed my youngest son's room, and he called me in. As we were lying on the bed, he said to me, "Mom and Chance aren't here now. Can I hear how you pray when you are alone?" But I couldn't pray, and I was totally crushed. Ducking into the bathroom, I sat down and cried—probably for the first time in decades. I was truly broken! Two days later I was fixing some boat equipment when a local pastor pulled into my driveway. I knew what he was going to say because he had broached the subject many times before. Each time I had managed to dodge it, but this time I was ready. The brokenness had readied my heart enough to accept the simple gospel message of God's grace.

At age 37, I finally surrendered. I came to faith in Jesus Christ and said a simple prayer, confessing with my mouth that Jesus is Lord and believing in my heart that God raised Him from the dead (Romans 10:9-10). I was born again.

Just as I finished my prayer, the grandfather clock chimed. That defining moment determined my destiny and changed the direction of my life—forever!

A man's heart plans his way,
but the LORD directs his steps.

PROVERBS 16:9

Chapter Two

Defining Moments That Determine Your Destiny

RON LINDNER

AS I SIT DOWN TO WRITE TODAY, I HAVE BEEN
on this earth for 80 years. A lot of water has passed under
the gunnels of my life.

Looking back, I can clearly see God's leading in my life
and in Al's. With closely shared dreams, visions, and ideals
encompassing a lifestyle career, we have enjoyed front-row
seats in each other's adventures, and we've shared many
defining moments.

Al calls them "God nudges." They are incidents in our
lives that we fully understand only when looking back
through the prism of time. We all have them in one form or

another. They are direct interventions that can come only from God and that turn our sails and chart a new course for our lives. Thinking back, all of us could probably write books chronicling the many twists and turns we've experienced—wins, losses, detours, and out-of-the-blue urgings from God.

One of our biggest God nudges transformed our careers and redirected 24 years of our lives.

The year was 1974, we had just sold our stakes in Lindy Tackle Company to Rayovac Corporation—a worldwide leader in battery power and innovation. At that time, it was part of a huge corporate conglomerate, and Al and I stayed on under a work contract in promotions, advertising, and merchandising.

A part of that contract included the continuation of *The Facts of Fishing*, an outdoor sport-fishing television series that we began in 1970 to promote our Lindy Tackle product line. With other industry sponsors on board, the show had already been on the air for five years and had gained a reputation as a popular and intense instructional angling program. Our unofficial motto was "Teaching America how to catch fish is our business." We had started with only a handful of stations, but by 1975, the series was aired on 25 upper-Midwest broadcast markets, including some pretty big ones.

Al was the primary host, and I was the secondary host. By this time, we had started to become well-known in the sport-fishing world. Al was easily recognizable with his distinctive sun-bleached hair and beard, tan skin, baseball cap with the black logo, plaid shirt, blue jeans, and moccasins. Folks would often stop to talk fishing with him at airports, boat landings, gas stations, and restaurants.

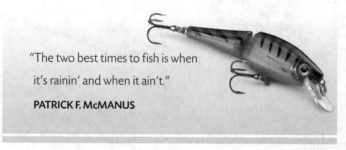

"The two best times to fish is when it's rainin' and when it ain't."

PATRICK F. McMANUS

Through the years, Al won two Bass Master tournaments and competed in a number of Bass Master Classics. Meanwhile, I penned countless instructional articles for many fishing publications and magazines. I also invented some lures that sold in the millions, and I concocted a number of other innovations that are still marketed today. So by 1975,

we had added quite a bit of experience to complement our résumés. With five years of television and all the other experiences under our belts, we both felt we were ready to branch out and produce our own television series.

Ted Turner was launching a new television broadcasting entity in Atlanta, Georgia. His vision would change the way people around the world received their television programming. I remember thinking he was going to shoot a thingamajig up into space and somehow bounce back a television show that would be caught by some kind of receiver dish and then be delivered into homes...wow!

Yes, WTBS Atlanta was planning to transmit some shows via satellite to cable systems and was hungry for more programming. The plan was to include movies, newscasts, cooking shows, sitcoms, talk shows, cartoons...even fishing and hunting shows. We made contact with executives at WTBS, and they liked what they saw—particularly that we were already airing in upper Midwest markets and had quite a following there. We left a meeting thinking we had an agreement in principle with a deal to be ironed out later. We definitely thought a contract was in the offing.

We hit the ground running. Al and I resigned our

positions at Rayovac, started to round up and sell sponsorships for this new television series, and began shopping for editing equipment and cameras. At this time, fishing television shows were still shot on film, and final postproduction was done in a studio, so it wasn't too expensive.

Then it happened.

Al was competing in a Bass Master tournament at Bull Shoals, Arkansas, when I received a call from Atlanta. Suddenly, our new show was going to be put on hold until some legal and other difficulties could be smoothed out.

For us this was like the kiss of death. We had gone way out on a limb, and now we were without jobs, without a television show, and without incomes! The news came too late for us to develop a new game plan for a network of broadcast stations for the upcoming year. Both of us had growing families and growing bills. We had to do something—fast!

Sick in spirit, I drove down to Arkansas to tell Al the bad news, praying he just might win a cash prize at the tournament to keep the wolves from the door. But to add to this desperate scenario, he had a bad finish and didn't win any money.

What happened next still boggles my mind, and it

amazed a number of people who witnessed or were part of a big-time God nudge.

To put things in perspective and to appreciate what happened, you should know that at this time, none of us had committed our lives to the Lord—not Al, me, or either of our wives. In fact, if you were to ask Al about Genesis, he might have asked if you were referring to a new spinning reel. I, on the other hand, had an academic interest and a rough knowledge of the Bible, but I had little understanding of the Bible's spiritual components. Both of our wives were wonderful women and mothers and were raised in nominal Christian households that held to the moral code of the times, yet they also knew very little of the working Spirit of God. For what it's worth, I did believe that if I really searched, God would somehow take care of me and mine.

Regardless of our spiritual condition, none of us was prepared for what was about to happen. Nor would we fully understand it until years later when we could look back and see the way God's amazing grace and mercy changed the trajectory of our lives.

Ron Lindner

Al and I had responsibilities. I had seven kids and Al had two. Our elderly parents lived with us as well—that makes 15 people to worry about. And at the time I was very, very worried.

During this same time, I was also troubled by my inability to deal with my alcoholism. I had been in AA for two years but was still having "slips," and I was desperately seeking solutions.

The first Scripture I heard and somewhat understood was Matthew 6:31,33—"Do not worry, saying, 'What shall we eat?' or 'What shall we drink?' or 'What shall we wear?'...But seek first the kingdom of God and His righteousness, and all these things shall be added to you."

When I read the words "seek first," I latched onto them, thinking I could seek God's kingdom and He would provide. Wow, what a deal! So I began to seek. Looking for spiritual answers, I began studying with various religious groups. Plenty of them existed in the 1970s, and some were way, way out in their beliefs. As it turned out, this part of my search was like that old song "Lookin' for Love (in All the Wrong Places)," and I would endure more visits to the house of pain with more bouts with alcohol before I learned the truth and simplicity of God's love.

Yet God in His wisdom knew something could be salvaged to His glory, and when we were on the verge of losing everything, little did we know that God evidently has a soft spot for fishermen.

A man's steps are of the LORD; how then can a man understand his own way?

PROVERBS 20:24

Chapter Three

But God...!

RON LINDNER

"MAN PROPOSES BUT GOD DISPOSES"—this line is from the fourteenth-century classic *Of the Imitation of Christ* by Thomas à Kempis. The thought is from Scripture: "There are many plans in a man's heart, nevertheless the LORD's counsel—that will stand" (Proverbs 19:21).

When reading the Scriptures, one cannot help but notice an oft-repeated expression—"But God..." In both the Old and New Testaments, it signals a change of perspective and a demonstration of God's absolute sovereignty. Al and I were about to experience a big change in direction and see our lives greatly impacted for the next 25 years and ultimately for eternity.

Even today the trip down to Bull Shoals, Arkansas, is still a bit of a fog. I can only remember parts of it. After I received the bad news from Atlanta that WTBS was not going to run our television shows for the coming season, I was in a manic state and started drinking heavily. Naturally I avoided going to any AA meetings. These were the days before cell phones, and I had to leave messages for Al to call me at my home. Only days later did he finally manage to call and speak to me. Meanwhile, my panic was rising.

Al called me from an outdoor pay phone with lots of background noise and a garbled reception. He had two days left in the tournament and was in no position or mood to talk, so he asked if we could finish the conversation after the tournament ended and he returned home. We ended our phone conversation, but I was in full-force panic mode. I had no faith in a good and loving God—nothing to rely on, nothing to calm me.

I was selfishly determined to share the bad news with Al regardless of how he felt or how it would affect his tournament play, so I decided to head south. I was going to see and talk to him no matter what. I also wanted to share with him a wild idea that I thought just might help to keep us afloat.

The entire trip down to Bull Shoals was motivated by my desperation and fear, and it turned out to be a complete waste of time and money. I muddled my way through a presentation to Al, but nothing was accomplished. Al and I were still out of business, and we had to do something—fast!

"There he stands, draped in more equipment than a telephone lineman, trying to outwit an organism with a brain no bigger than a breadcrumb, and getting licked in the process."

PAUL O'NEILL

When we got home, I sobered up, began attending regular AA meetings again, and eventually became clearheaded. I explained to Al, Mary, and Dolores the full scope of our dilemma and my out-of-the-blue solution. As it would turn out, my solution wasn't mine at all. It was God's way of nudging us toward His plans for our lives, including a series of events we could not have imagined in our wildest dreams.

As the situation stood, we wouldn't be back on television for at least two years, maybe longer. And we still had no idea what the business heads in Atlanta were going to do.

During that interim, I proposed we write a fishing study guide—an in-depth course on angling education. This was my so-called bright idea. These Study Reports, which I started calling them, would reveal some of our secrets and explain to the fishing world our "Algebra of Angling"— something we developed in the previous years during our many barnstorming tours.

In these Study Reports we would give the fishing world a detailed look at some of our little-known insights, tricks, and tips. We could unveil and promote this venture in our ongoing "Fishing Facts" magazine articles that we were providing pro bono. I figured we might make $15,000 in a year—maybe even more. And if we continued sport-show and seminar appearances as well as anything else that came our way, we could somehow stay afloat and get a television show going again in the future.

To keep all of this in perspective, in 1975 the average annual income was $10,450. Gas was 57¢ a gallon. You could buy a decent new home for $40,000, and a new Chevy cost $4000.

At this point Al still had a little money left from our sale of Lindy Tackle, but that was going fast. Neither of us had received a paycheck for many months. Al was still tournament fishing and would continue for a few more years. He had a few sponsors, but the cash prizes were small, and expenses were big. He was still booked steadily on the seminar circuit, and this could bring in a few dollars, but the main sport show season was already over. Al had some breathing room left, but I was quickly going broke.

After a few payments on my house, everything would be gone. I needed an infusion of cash. I considered looking for jobs with tackle companies or working on road-building survey crews, as I had done in Chicago. I thought that after a wonderful decade, our dream was coming to an end.

But God…!

Perhaps no one was more surprised than me when Al and our wives bought into the Study Report package I proposed. None of us had any experience in publishing, subscription solicitation, or acquisition. Yet we agreed to prepare a brochure, mail it out, and hopefully get a thousand rabid fishing

fans to bite on the $15 subscription offer—very pricy for the time. Over the years, we had accumulated a mailing list of about 40,000 names. Mary and Dolores eagerly volunteered to type up thousands of mailing labels. They were busy pounding away on our old manual typewriters for weeks.

Some years prior to this, I did a very big favor for George Pazik, publisher of *Fishing Facts* magazine at that time. In return he let me mail through his list for free. At the time, it numbered about 160,000 names. (Who says doing favors for people doesn't pay off later?)

We had just enough money to purchase a bulk mailing permit and the pending postage for half of the 200,000-piece mailing. A local printer that we worked a lot with during our tenure at Lindy Tackle Company printed the brochure "on spec"—we shook hands with the agreement to pay for the printing costs in three months. All of this was a long shot to say the least.

But God…!

We dribbled the early mailings out in order to get some cash flow for the later mailings. The stream of subscriptions began as a trickle…then grew into a steady flow…and then turned into a torrent! We immediately saw that we would probably get more than the one thousand $15 subscribers we had originally hoped for. In fact, in the first five weeks we had 10,000 prepaid subscribers. Our mailbox was filled with checks, money orders, and cash totaling $150,000. No "bill me laters" or credit cards to be processed—just money that we didn't owe to a bank or any creditor other than the subscribers.

In 1975, $150,000 was the equivalent of $750,000 today. That's right, three-quarters of a million dollars. We were all stunned. In a couple of months, all 200,000 pieces were mailed. We had nearly 17,000 subscribers and $255,000 in responses by the year's end.

In today's money, we had the equivalent of a million dollars—cash!

Impossible? Yes!

But God…!

REFLECTION

Ron Lindner

At this point, the idea of publishing a magazine had never occurred to any of us. However, in time the study guides would somehow morph into a magazine. Originally the study guides did not have any advertising. They were what they were—Study Reports, very detailed and very in-depth. The story of how and why the Study Reports became a magazine would fill another book.

The magazine would eventually become a launching pad for all sorts of other business ventures. What grew from a flagship publication base of operation would include books, DVDs, species-specific magazines, a television series, on-the-water schools, and a professional walleye tournament circuit complete with its own magazine and television series. We would also produce a daily three-minute instructional angling segment that would air on 900 radio stations. The personal appearances by our burgeoning staff were beyond count.

All of this was the outgrowth of a God nudge. In the course of these adventures, we would become born again. God's miraculous hand would be displayed not only in our lives but also in the many lives with which we were interacting. For example, we eventually began the Fishers of Men Retreats, which enabled us to introduce thousands of men to Jesus throughout the years.

I'm confident this was part of what God had in mind when He took us from where we thought we were going to where He wanted us to be. At the time I thought the loss of an immediate television contract was a catastrophe. But it wasn't—it was a blessing.

During that interim, Lindy Tackle / Rayovac had recorded enough shows to continue featuring Al through the 1977 season. In 1978 and 1979, we were privileged to work with the famed outdoor film producer Glenn Lau. We also had a segment on the

Coors *Western Outdoorsmen* television series, which included other show hosts destined to become legends of the industry, including Roland Martin, Rick Clunn, and Homer Circle.

Interestingly, we never aired on WTBS in Atlanta. However, in God's infinite grace and provision, He has enabled us to air on television every year for 45 years (as of 2015) without missing a single season.

But God…!

For as the heavens are higher than the earth,
so are My ways higher than your ways,
and My thoughts than your thoughts.

ISAIAH 55:9

Chapter Four

When It's God's Best, It's Always Better

AL LINDNER

FACING UNCERTAINTY IN ANY ENDEAVOR CAN be daunting. Whether you're leaving home for the first time or launching into business for yourself, once you step out into the big unknown, the alarm bells can ring loud and often. Some folks say they enjoy the challenge, but most of us find it a bit unnerving.

Every spring season for many years, Ron and I aired a series of television fishing shows on a host of Midwestern broadcast markets. We styled the format around what we were comfortable with, and it worked very successfully. But in 1984, satellite and cable television began transforming our industry. We knew that patterns, syndication methodology, and cost of airtime were all in a state of flux. If we failed to make a move, our show would wither and die on the vine.

Our first step was to take our situation to God. Praying with Ron and with Mike Simpson, who worked with us in television, we dedicated the new program to God and asked for His grace and guidance and a blessing on our labors.

Then we began contacting every satellite and cable outlet that might offer our type of show. Based on the good reputation and prominence we had gained as well as the awards we had garnered for our program, we thought we would be welcomed with open arms.

"We may say of angling as Dr. Boteler said of strawberries: 'Doubtless God could have made a better berry, but doubtless God never did'; and so, if I may be judge, God never did make a more calm, quiet, innocent recreation than angling."

IZAAK WALTON, *THE COMPLEAT ANGLER*

I flew to ESPN in New York full of confidence, but I couldn't even get a hearing in the Big Apple. Mike went to CBN, where he had some contacts, but they weren't interested either. Ron made his pitch to TBS, WGN, USA and Discovery. All of it netted absolutely nothing!

It was baffling—every door had slammed shut. Little by little our confidence turned to anxiety as fear and doubt began to take root.

We kept searching and found that TNN, the Nashville Network, was beginning to gain cable outlets and satellite viewership. Its demographic focus was right for us—downhome people who would be interested in fishing. We also met several Christians in key positions at TNN and their satellite business, the Grand Ole Opry, who made us feel very comfortable. But TNN's audience reach at that time, when compared to ESPN, USA, CBN, or TBS, was minuscule. With our options running out, we resigned ourselves to the situation and cut a deal.

Still, plenty of questions loomed in our minds. We had prayed hard for guidance and God's blessing, but the stations that reached bigger audiences, which we felt we needed to make the show a success, gave us the cold shoulder. All we

ended up with was a small cable outlet focusing on country music. Though we were very disappointed, we decided to give it our best and hope that something better would come along. I don't recall that we even thanked God at the time for opening the door at TNN.

Fast-forward a decade.

TNN experienced astonishing growth, and so did we. In fact, during one particular year, *In-Fisherman TV* was seen by more viewers than any other television fishing show on earth. And on top of that, during these phenomenal growth years, the In-Fisherman media network of magazines, radio, books, videos, and tournaments was established as a nationwide entity.

Do we serve an awesome God who answers prayers, or what?

REFLECTION

Ron Lindner

In retrospect, God could not have answered our prayers better than by putting us on TNN when He did. As the world of satellite and cable networks shook out, it was absolutely the best outlet for our show at the time. God knows well in advance what is best for His children. The older I get, the more I realize that what might look in the short term to be a stingy response or even a "no" answer is always, in the final analysis, the right thing in the right place at the right time.

Whoever confesses Me before men,
him will I also confess before My Father
who is in heaven.

MATTHEW 10:32

Chapter Five

The Fish Symbol

AL LINDNER

OF ALL THE THINGS WE HAVE PRINTED OR
aired on television over the years, the one that has prompted
the most heart-searching questions, comments, and opinions was our fish symbol. For us it has a long and hallowed
history.

In the early fall of 1983, I returned to my office after a
day on the water to check my mail. I was surprised to find
an order for a full-page ad in an upcoming holiday issue
of our fishing magazine. It was from one of America's top
producers and distributors of alcoholic beverages. When
we had pursued this type of advertising previously, we were

told our circulation was too small, but now the opportunity we had waited for was right in my hands. The full-page ad was tastefully done, extolling the joys of the season and featuring a picture-perfect Christmas tree with beautiful gift-wrapped presents beneath. In the lower right corner was a very small image of their iconic bottle with their prestigious brand name next to it.

Our magazine was eight years old at the time, and we had more than 150,000 subscribers. We had been on the news-stands for a few years, primarily around the upper Midwest, and every publisher at the time coveted alcohol and tobacco ads. Besides paying top dollar, these ads signaled to ad agencies that a publication had "arrived," and new ads for similar competitive products often followed. Usually these companies ran a series of ads that were like "found money" for us— money that didn't come from the endemic tourism, boat, motor, rod, reel, and lure advertisers we regularly serviced. These ads also opened doors for commercials for our television and radio shows. This was a very big deal!

To put my reaction to the ad into perspective, I need to give a bit of family background. By this time, Ron, Dolores, and Mary had been believers for a few years. I had

just accepted Jesus as my Savior six months earlier. I was immersed in the Bible, and each day brought a new revelation for me.

Back then, the Christian fish symbol was not displayed nearly as widely as it is today. An occasional bumper sticker was about all you were likely to see. A year earlier, Dolores had read Deuteronomy 6:9—"Write them on the doorposts of your house and on your gates"—so she put a fish symbol on their mailbox at home. Seeing it, Ron decided to put one on his boat as well. That was it, and no one thought much more about it.

But during that year, Ron had dabbled with it more and more, adding a cross to the fish and trying some variations in conjunction with our logo. A few months before receiving the ad, Ron, Dolores, Mary, and I had met and agreed that we would put the words, "Jesus Is Lord" over the entry of our building. When the sign was mounted, we held hands and prayed, dedicating our company to God. With that dedication, we also decided to add the fish symbol to our corporate logo, which involved a vast amount of changes on printing plates, artwork, preprinted materials, patches, jackets, hats, and so on.

So with all this going on, I looked at the ad and felt what some Christians would call a check in my spirit. Others would call it a strong gut feeling that something isn't quite right.

Make no mistake about it—we were struggling during these years. We needed the money immediately, and this ad could open the gates to a lot more similar revenue. This infusion of capital could very well take us to the next level. And the ad was in no way offensive. We had run boat ads with bikini-clad models that were far less tasteful. So I thought to myself, *What's your problem with this ad? Are you turning into a prude or something?* Still, I wasn't comfortable with running the ad.

So I called together a family business meeting—the first one that included Dolores and Mary. Before this, Ron or I would make a decision, and that was it. I showed them the ad, and our wives immediately gave it the thumbs-down. They, however, didn't have to go out and peddle ad space. Then Ron said he was leaning in their direction. I confess I was torn. Ron finally said that since I was in charge of advertising, I should make the final call.

That night I prayed and pondered it. How would we

draw the line on ads? Should we even try? Is there a difference between bad taste and bad morals? What about smokeless chew tobacco and cheeky bikini-themed boat ads? How about ads for real-estate hustlers?

Something else was involved here. The fish symbol was beginning to go on all our materials, including our media kits. Would some of our key sales outlets get offended, thinking we were getting self-righteous about ads? We really couldn't afford to lose an occasional subscriber, let alone be regarded as religious kooks by the big ad agencies and firms that provided our primary income.

Those questions bombarded my mind. Would we ever grow beyond a narrow-niche fishing magazine and regional television fishing show if we painted ourselves into such a tight corner?

That night I read Proverbs 16:3 (NLT): "Commit your actions to the LORD, and your plans will succeed." It was clear to me that we had committed ourselves when we first displayed the fish symbol, and now it was equally clear that it was time to put our money where our mouth was. I knew I had my answer, and a peace followed.

The next morning I told Ron of my decision, and then

I had to tell our advertising account executives. This would impact their sales commissions, and needless to say, they were not happy. From that point on, we made it our policy not to take any alcohol or tobacco ads—no exceptions. If anything else that was questionable came up, we would consider it on a case-by-case basis.

This was a defining moment. From then on it seemed as if everything we touched turned to gold. Our entire company flourished in every direction, and the magazine circulation and advertising revenues rocketed. Over the ensuing months, we received more ads from new accounts than we ever had before. Lots more! We even got ads from firms we had a hard time cracking before—and all were perfectly acceptable.

There is no question in my mind that this was a confirmation from God that we were on the right track. And despite criticism and difficulties, we've never had a moment's regret. The public display of the fish symbol reminds us that we are to depend on God as our source and not look to any other place or to anyone else.

REFLECTION

Dolores Lindner

When we sold our business to a New York publishing conglomerate, things naturally changed. The fish and cross came off the logo, and "Jesus Is Lord" came off the doorway. And well they should because these were our personal statements. Still, I cannot help but remember how blessed I was the first time we used the fish and cross on our television sign-off. And every time the show closed, this symbol reminded me that God was truly our provider.

Over the years our company has been honored and blessed with many awards, trophies, and mementos. But when we left the company, the "Jesus Is Lord" sign and the fish symbol etched in glass on an entry window were the first things we took with us.

Jesus was right—where your treasure is, there your heart is also.

*All Scripture is God-breathed and is useful
for teaching, rebuking, correcting and training in
righteousness, so that the servant of God may be
thoroughly equipped for every good work.*

2 TIMOTHY 3:16-17 NIV

Chapter Six

Thoroughly Equipped

RON LINDNER

WHEN IT COMES TO SPORT FISHING, I LIVE BY
the old Boy Scout rule, "Be prepared." For me that includes
arranging a complete array of lures and paraphernalia in the
boat with solutions for all fishing eventualities and possibil-
ities. That's my rule.

At an annual charity fundraising bass tournament held
by former Minnesota Viking coach Dennis Green, I discovered a new life lesson about being "thoroughly equipped."
It was a team event, and I was with a good friend who is
both a professional tournament angler and a believer. The

tournament was early in the season, so we decided to check the shallows for pre-spawn and spawning largemouth during the pre-fishing.

On the first practice day we found a wind-protected bay that had warmed early and had the right bottom content to attract staging fish. We skirted the shoreline and scanned the water not only for fish but also for the telltale signs of use, such as swept nests and log brushings. It wasn't long before we came upon a dead giveaway—yellowish plate-size depressions all over the shallows. We didn't make a cast, but merely noted the spots and kept on looking.

Leaving this area, we also fished a number of other locations and patterns—specifically, staging bass on two large, weedy flats on the main lake. Careful not to "burn" these spots, we caught just enough fish on spinner baits to indicate the numbers of bass present. By the end of the second day of pre-fishing, we had our game plan in place. If we drew an early flight, we would fish the small protected bay. But if we drew a later flight, we would head for the large main flats, figuring the small bay would be jammed with boats.

Well, we drew number 90, which put us at the back of the pack. Going directly to the flats, we caught fish and limited out by noon, but most of the fish were "buck bass" (around two pounds). Winning the tournament would require fish larger than three pounds, and we were confounded at not being able to move up. So we ran here and there, trying to upgrade our catch with the same spinner baits. Late in the afternoon when we were on the way back to the weigh-in site, we stopped in the small spawning bay. No one was there, but that wasn't strange. We were in the last flight, and most of the other boats had already headed back. Nonetheless, we decided to put the troll motor down and make a quick pass with the spinner baits.

"Even a bad day of fishing is better than a good day of work."

UNKNOWN

Suddenly, bang, bang, bang, we caught three fish. Not monsters, but large enough to cull three of our fish up, and they were the largest we caught all day. With time running out, we headed back to the weigh-in site. After weighing

in, we went to the scoreboard, which was flanked by all the contestants. A big bag of fish, averaging almost three and three-quarter pounds per fish, was leading, and the team that brought it in eventually won the tournament.

After the event, we got together with the other players in a time-honored post-tournament tradition and indulged ourselves in some "coulda, woulda, shoulda" talk. The small spawning bay put up the winning fish, and the first-place team caught them "dead sticking" soft, plastic worms. The fish in the bay apparently did not turn on until afternoon, after most of the early boats had left.

The winners pretty much had the bay and fish all to themselves. They had left shortly before we arrived and had upgraded right till the end. The presentation was a slow, almost motionless retrieve. The big fish simply did not want anything that was moving quickly.

With this news, my tournament partner and I eyed each other, and the recriminations started. How could such an obvious solution escape us? We both love dead sticking and pride ourselves in being good at it. With my boat locker filled with an arsenal of lures, why didn't we even try soft plastic ones? We knew about the solution, and we had the

equipment and experience to use it well, but we failed to employ it. We concluded that we simply fell into a rut with the spinner baits.

On the three-hour drive back home after the tournament, I mulled things over my head and chided myself for missing the dead-stick pattern. It struck me how similar this was to other situations in my life in which I have failed to use all the spiritual equipment God has given me. As a result, I missed God's best or suffered needlessly.

REFLECTION

Al Lindner

I am constantly amazed by the many ways God meets us and how often He communicates through what we are familiar with. God has often used lures, rods, and boats to teach us fishing-related lessons we can easily identify with. The psalmist David had been a shepherd, and he understood God's goodness in terms of green pastures and still waters. The apostle Peter, an experienced fisherman, knew that God supplies all our needs and can even put a coin in a fish's mouth to help him out. Recently, I read a book by an astrophysicist who came to understand the workings of God through "heat-releasing radioisotopes," "mesospheric ozone," and "supernovae emissions."

Because God loves us, He wants us to be familiar with His Word (the Scriptures). If we listen closely, we can hear Him speaking to us in His still, small voice deep inside.

Do not live according to the flesh but according to the spirit.

ROMANS 8:4 NIV

Chapter Seven

When the Flesh Gets the Upper Hand

RON LINDNER

ONE LESSON I HAD TO LEARN—AND LESSONS like this one are always costly—was to never let my emotions make decisions for me.

Long ago, we were involved in a lawsuit that regarded a very complex trademark and copyright issue with complications that ran back almost 20 years. As a general rule, the Scripture warns us to stay out of the courts if at all possible, and over the years we heeded that counsel. The Scripture also plainly tells us that brothers in the Lord should never go to court against each other (1 Corinthians 6:1-7). But in this case, there was a question regarding who owned

a specific copyright. We were called into court and forced to defend ourselves.

"Catch-and-release fishing is a lot like golf. You don't have to eat the ball to have a good time."

UNKNOWN

This is where things started to go amiss. Right from the start, I took the suit very personally. I wasn't mature in the faith yet, and that led to big errors in judgment. Although I prayed about it in a general way, I let some bad feelings create an atmosphere of ongoing confrontation. I personally felt unjustly attacked and thought, *We're being played for a patsy. If they think we're just going to stand there and take a slap in the face, they have another thing coming. If they want a fight, that's what they'll get…*and it lasted for more than four horrible, agonizing years. As litigation unfolded and several law firms, insurance companies, and jurisdictions became involved, the lawsuit absorbed all my time and energy as only litigation of this kind can. It began to take on a life of

its own. I was caught hook, line, and sinker, and I'm sure the devil played me like a small crappie on a musky rod.

I made a second mistake as well. I knew this battle involved spiritual warfare, but I did not fully put on the whole armor of God (Ephesians 6:10-18). I did not pray with all types of prayer or with persistent supplication. I could have done many things spiritually, but I didn't. And the longer this ordeal went on, the more fleshly the fight became for me. Were our attorneys making progress? Were they doing enough, and would they counter the opposition's legal tricks? Was the judge going to give us a summary judgment? Why couldn't people see the facts?

I was depending on worldly things that can't really be trusted.

Finally, when everyone involved got fed up with the whole mess, I started to truly pray for the opposition (this wasn't easy for me). I wasn't praying that they would see the error of their ways and that we could find an equitable compromise. Instead, I started praying for their well-being and for their families—especially for their little ones. This was the closest I could get to expressing the agape love that the Scripture plainly tells us never fails (1 Corinthians 13:8).

Surprise, surprise…soon after I began praying this way, we received word that the primary suit had been settled in our favor. But by now there were suits and countersuits. Next we heard that the other suit also looked favorable for us. At this point I made a phone call to the executive of the other company. This was our first contact since the suit started, and both of us had been advised (indeed chided) by the attorneys not to do this. Nonetheless, I asked for a lunch with him alone, and he accepted. Forty-five minutes later we shook hands and left the problem behind us, except for the mounds of paperwork to close it out legally. It was finally over!

Al Lindner

As the lawsuit droned on and on ad nauseam, our conference room became known as the war room. Instead of brimming with creative ideas and positive energy, it was littered with legal documents, depositions, and lawyers' briefs. Ron's days and nights were consumed by the lawsuit, and he had to neglect a lot of his day-to-day business. The whole mess wasted an enormous amount of time, money, and energy.

As things unfolded, we both fell into a trap. Yes, both of us failed to use all the spiritual equipment God had supplied for us. Instead, we relied on flesh-and-blood tactics, and that's always a mistake.

All the pressure created a toxic atmosphere as only this type of court proceeding can. Today, neither of us would fall for this obvious ploy by the enemy to steal our peace. In fact, not so long ago we had the opportunity to engage in another legal battle, but in prayer, both of us received assurance that we were not to open that door. Individually, we were led to Jesus's words "Shake the dust off your feet" (Luke 9:5). Yes, the Scriptures provide the wisdom we need to avoid fleshly entanglements. We've never been to court since.

Whatever you do, work at it with all your heart, as working for the Lord, not for human masters.

COLOSSIANS 3:23 NIV

Chapter Eight

Don't Look for Answers in the Devil's Gap

RON LINDNER

WITH ITS ALMOST ONE MILLION SPRAWLING acres and 14,000 islands, Lake of the Woods on the Minnesota–Ontario border sports some intriguing names for its areas—Dead Man's Portage, the Corkscrew, the Bowling Alley, the Tangle, and Fall Dangerous. Then there are two even more ominous sounding places—the Devil's Gap and Hades. Those two are forever etched in my memory.

In the early 1990s, I finally had an opportunity to fish a bass tournament with my eldest son, Bill. Though a renowned wildlife, fish, and food photographer, and one of the best all-around multispecies anglers I know, Bill was no

fan of competitive fishing. For years I badgered him to be my tournament partner, but he would always shrug his shoulders and say, "I'm too high-strung for this kind of thing."

But after many years of working for a major book-publishing firm, Bill decided to strike out on his own as a freelance photographer, and he needed a fair chunk of money to purchase some specialized photography equipment. I told him that if he'd be my fishing partner for the Kenora Bass International (KBI) and if we won, he could keep the entire purse. In this 227-boat field, the first-place prize was $50,000 (Canadian), and even second- and third-place finishes paid fairly well. To my pleasant surprise, Bill agreed.

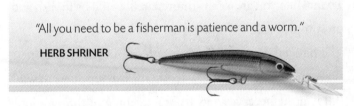

"All you need to be a fisherman is patience and a worm."

HERB SHRINER

I thought that during the tournament, I might be able to share some wisdom on how to run his new business. The way we plan and prepare and execute the strategy to fish a tournament relates directly to business. For example, poorly maintained equipment or sloppy time management can beat you in a fishing tournament as easily as in a photo shoot. I also hoped Bill would always incorporate a spiritual dimension in his photography business, just as we would ask God for help and guidance in the tournament. As I always do, we would pray together for safety—not only for us but for all competitors.

I believe that in a tournament or any other competitive sport, God usually lets normal events unfold unless He has a sovereign reason to do otherwise. The best-prepared competitor usually wins the event. In fishing tournaments, contestants must do their homework and pre-fish. To skip those vital steps, say a fast prayer, and expect God to bless you with a win when you are totally unprepared would be foolish and presumptuous.

So together we set out about pre-fishing in dead earnest. Over and over we said to each other, "We came here to win!" Bill had the necessary raw fishing talent, and through long experience I knew tournament fishing tactics and strategies that lead to wins.

As we pre-fished, a pattern slowly began to emerge. We

found that big smallmouth hung along the chains of the buoys that mark the many rocky shoals of the lake. We were not targeting the shoals as much as the chains and buoys adjacent to them. Many of the fish were sitting right under the buoys themselves. When we would run and gun the 32-buoy milk route, we would get about nine bites a day—not a lot of fish, but they were all big. If we could boat six fish of this size on both days of the tournament, we knew we could win. We had also found a number of smaller fish concentrated in two places I mentioned earlier—Hades and the Devil's Gap.

After four days of practice, we were definitely "on fish, and big fish." Our game plan was set, and all we had to do was implement it by the numbers. I had never felt more confident in a tournament and never have since. In fact, we might have been a little cocky.

The first day went just as planned. We first went for smaller fish to fill out our limit, and then we culled them out with fewer but bigger fish along the buoys. By day's end, we were in third place and just ten ounces off that big-money, first-place prize!

The second and final day, however, we opted not to go

for the smaller fish. We needed six big fish to make up for our weight deficit, so why waste time? We started working the buoys right off the bat, but an overnight cold front had blown through, switching the wind to the northwest. It was blowing hard right down the alleys of the markers we were fishing. The water temperature had dropped, and the bass were really slow.

We took an hour and a half to boat our first fish, but it was a lunker! An hour and a half later and countless markers behind us, we caught a second big fish. By noon we had only three of the six fish we needed. Then another long lull set in as the wind increased and the whitecaps tossed us about, making the boat hard to handle.

By one o'clock we were stuck with only three fish, and the alarm bells of doubt started to clang. With a three p.m. flight weigh-in, we had until two thirty to leave this area and avoid being disqualified. In my heart, I was asking God why the stinking wind, why now of all times, why not from the other direction, and why right down the chute where we needed to fish? Hadn't we worked hard? Hadn't we worked smart?

At one fifteen I said to Bill, "Let's go to Hades or Devil's

Gap and try for our limit with a few smaller fish. A smaller check is better than nothing."

From a purely professional tournament angler's viewpoint, this was good strategy. But Bill looked straight at me and said, "We came here to win." Minutes later we caught the fourth fish—a biggie. But by two fifteen we didn't have another hit, so I mentioned Hades or Devil's Gap again.

Bill shook his head and said, "Let's just stay with it."

Five minutes later, Bill caught our fifth fish—another good-sized one, pushing my roller-coaster confidence on the upswing again. With fifteen minutes left and thinking out loud, I said to Bill, "God's guidance had us stay with it. We'll get that last fish soon." But as I watched the last minutes tick down, I knew that if there was heavy boat congestion in the channel, we might not even make it in time.

I finally told Bill, "We gotta go!"

We bailed with one fish short of the limit. I felt totally dejected and began the old second-guessing game. We should have gone to Hades for a small bass so we could at least net a decent check and save face with a limit.

Flying down the lake at top speed, we made it to the weigh-in area with five minutes to spare. In the distance I could see the continuous lines of boats racing toward the finish line. Then, glancing to my left, I saw a rock sticking out of the water along the shoreline where I'd had a strike but missed the fish during the practice days.

Acting on impulse, I maneuvered toward the rock and cut the engine. Bobbing in the water without power, I didn't even put the trolling motor down. I struggled to get my balance and grabbed the first rod I could get free, flipped the jig out to the rock, and immediately felt weight on the end. Thinking I was hung up, I yanked not once but twice, hoping to free the lure. Suddenly a big smallie leapt four feet high out of the water!

Both Bill and I were stunned. Bill stumbled to his feet and fumbled to get the net loose from the tie-down. With the trolling motor still strapped down and the wind blowing, we were bouncing all over in the waves. Fighting the fish up and back and under the boat, I somehow got the fish near enough for Bill to lean over and net the fish with one lightning stab.

Knowing we had but seconds left, I dropped the rod and put the fish in the live well with the line and lure still in his mouth. We raced to the finish line and made it in with thirty seconds to spare.

Coming off plane, I looked at Bill, who was grinning from ear to ear, and confidently said, "We just won the tournament."

And we did—by three ounces! Suddenly all those small fish in Hades and Devil's Gap looked very small.

REFLECTION

Ron Lindner

Later, as I was in prayer and meditation, the Lord spoke to my heart and said, "Would the win have been any sweeter if you had caught all the fish in the first hour? Would you have learned anything? When things don't go as smooth as you think they should, your faith wavers and you grasp for easy solutions—usually your own solutions and usually in the wrong places. Jonah and Abraham did the same. Instead of staying with what you know is right, you bail for quick fixes like the Devil's Gap or Hades, and you settle for much less than what could have been."

Between the KBI and the allied Canadian Rainy Lake Tournament, we've racked up many top-ten finishes and had fun doing it. Bill went on to win two more very prestigious and high-paying tournaments with his brother James in Canada.

There is a way that seems right to a man,
but its end is the way of death.

PROVERBS 14:12

Chapter Nine

When God Opens the Door, Go Through It

RON LINDNER

SPENDING A LIFETIME ON OCEANS, SEAS, lakes, rivers, and reservoirs, I've had countless occasions to ride out big waves and strong winds, and I've been spooked by lightning strikes nearby. But I've never been truly frightened, and I've had relatively few harrowing ordeals—such as this one.

I was fishing a bass tournament on Lake Minnetonka, a 16,000-acre lake in Minnesota that's broken up into numerous small, interconnecting bays. During the pre-fishing phase, I was working alone as the sweltering heat and humidity of early summer worsened in the afternoon. The forecast was for thunderstorms, but it didn't take a weatherman to predict that. The air was downright oppressive. The gray gulls and geese that abound on this waterway had already vanished.

Suddenly the fish "turned on," as they often do in weather like this. A cold front pushing through seems to trigger the bass to feed before the storm. A huge black cloud had rolled up like a wall on the western horizon, and I could hear the constant rumble of thunder in the distance. Knowing I had a fast boat and was close to the landing, I hoped to find one more concentration of bass along the weed line before I made a run for it.

Suddenly the black clouds, some dipping ominously, were coming straight at me. Lightning ignited the sky, and thunder boomed everywhere. An eerie yellow-green light descended on the landscape. With a blast of cold air, the wind picked up. It was time to bail and boogie.

To my consternation, as I turned the key on my 150-horse motor, it sputtered a number of times before finally turning over. Idling out through the narrows, I spied a large, canopied boat dock with long wooden pilings that was sheltered by a big hill. A large cabin cruiser was moored there with an open slip right next to it—a perfect refuge from the strong winds.

I hesitated momentarily at this open invitation but then thought, *At 60 miles an hour, I can make it back to the landing, walk to the restaurant, have some iced tea, and make a couple phone calls*. Without delay, I jacked up the motor, slammed down the throttle, and blasted off, ignoring the nearby dock and disregarding the lake's speed limit.

As I careened around a point, I realized how badly I had miscalculated the speed of the storm. Under a black wall of angry-looking, low-hanging clouds, I was slammed by rain, wind, and huge waves. At the speed I was going when I hit the first wave, my 19-foot bass boat went airborne. Simultaneously, a blast of refrigerated wind caught me in midair and threw the boat on its side. Landing with a bone-jarring bang, I almost flew out, barely able to hang on to the steering wheel.

In the process, I speared a large wave with the nose of the boat. As the deluge swept over the front deck, it tore loose the front-mounted depth finder and the safety strap on the troll motor. A piece of debris, perhaps the depth finder, hit the side of my face and knocked off my prescription sunglasses.

Somehow the boat righted itself, and the engine kept running. I scrambled for my life jacket but realized it was buried in the lockers under boxes of lures, rods, and other fishing gear. Without my glasses and with cold sheets of water and mothball-size hail beating down on me, I fumbled to hit the bilge pump switch on the dashboard. Click... click...click—nothing!

The cockpit was now shin deep with rising water. I knew I had to get the boat moving and "on plane," and I did. Advancing toward the landing dock, I saw a flotilla of craft crowded everywhere. They too were caught short by the storm, leaving no room for me to dock there. Suddenly, the boat started a foreboding list.

Relentless sheets of rain continued to obscure my vision, and I knew my last shot for shelter was a canal nearby with a bridge. If I could get under the bridge and out of the rain, I might be able to get the bilge pump running. But as I got closer to the bridge, I saw a number of boats piled side to side, and my boat was listing dangerously. My only alternative was to beach the boat, but both sides of the canal's entrance were lined four feet high with huge rocks.

I pushed the throttle, but the list was so bad I could no

longer power the boat. I knew it was going down. As the craft dipped, I scampered up the side like a sailor on a torpedoed ship, jumped off, and swam toward shore. The old "this can't be happening to me" refrain went through my mind. Then the boat "turtled," flipping upside down, half underwater.

As I stood in waist-deep water, soaked to the bone and shivering cold, I was proof of the old mariner saying that was fashioned after the apostle Paul's storm saga in Acts 27: "The sea is unforgiving of stupidity." Once I pulled away from that protected dock, I pushed myself out from under God's protective umbrella and paid the price. Eventually, my boat was recovered at great cost, and it never ran well again. I hope I learned my lesson.

Al Lindner

This same storm struck the US Open golf champion-ship at Hazeltine National Golf Club outside Min-neapolis. One spectator was killed and five others were injured, one seriously, when they were hit by lightning.

When God opens a door in your life, don't ever pass it by. I'm sure God saved Ron that spot at the covered dock that tragic day, but Ron thought he had a better way—his way. Doors open, and doors close…some-times forever. The laws of God's kingdom are every bit as certain in their operation as the laws of the wind and rain, and if we stubbornly refuse what He provides in His grace and love, we will reap the consequences. The decision of a moment can determine one's whole future. A time comes to every person when he must follow God's leading or refuse His provision. May we be quick to go through the doors He opens and never miss the precious gifts He has for each of us.

The thief does not come except to steal, and to kill, and to destroy. I have come that they may have life, and that they may have it more abundantly.

JOHN 10:10

Chapter Ten

Expect a Good Report

AL LINDNER

I REMEMBER THE MOMENT I RECEIVED THE phone call from Mary. It was a Friday night in July 1997, and I was alone in my motel room. I had been fishing the Canadian Bass Championship on Rainy Lake.

"Al," she spoke slowly, "the mammogram I took on Wednesday showed a lump on my breast. The doctor has scheduled me for surgery on Tuesday morning at seven." It took a while for her words sink in, but when they finally did, I felt their force and was glad I was sitting down.

My first response was, "Mary, let's pray," which we did. And then I said, "I'm packing up and coming home right

away." Mary's response was as calm as the evening lake. "No," she said. "Stay and fish the tournament. There's really nothing you can do here, and I'll be just fine." We talked for a while and prayed again before saying goodbye. Then I took a long walk…with God. We needed to talk, and I had a lot on my heart. By the time I was nearly back to my room, I felt a peace begin to come over me. As I crossed the parking lot of a tire store near the motel, I heard the Lord's still, small voice deep in my being: "Don't worry. Mary will be okay."

With that amazing reassurance, I finished the tournament on Sunday and immediately headed home. That evening and all day Monday, Mary was amazingly calm. She went about her normal routine, read healing Scriptures, listened to tapes, and claimed 1 Peter 2:24 out loud: "By his stripes I am healed and whole." That's my Mary.

"It's a done deal. I'll be fine," she said, recalling a song we sing in church that declares, "We will believe the report of the Lord!" So Mary's response to the doctor was always the same: "I'm expecting a good report!"

Early Tuesday morning we arrived at the hospital along with one of our pastors. He and I laid hands on Mary and prayed for her, and then the nurses wheeled her out to the surgery room. Forty-five minutes later the doctor came out.

"Mary's lump was cancerous," he said. "We cut it out along with twelve lymph nodes, which have been sent to Minneapolis. We should have the report back on Thursday."

I was stunned momentarily. This was not the good report I was expecting. But again, the peace of God came over my heart, and I felt the words deep in my being: "She'll be okay."

As I went into the recovery room, the doctor was telling Mary the lump was cancerous. Again, she looked at me, smiled, and said, "I'll be just fine, Al. I'm expecting a good report."

Mary was checked out of the hospital on Wednesday, and as we drove home she was all smiles—praising God and laughing! She hadn't even taken a pain pill yet. (I would have taken the whole bottle by then.) To her the surgery was no worse than a trip to the dentist to get a tooth filled. She reassured me, "Honey, I'm fine."

That night Mary slept on a recliner. She still had a drain tube attached, and the recliner provided the only comfortable sleeping position.

I went to bed alone, unsure of what I might be facing. For the first time, doubt and fear came over me like a heavy blanket. I had the craziest, most ominous thoughts imaginable—thoughts only the author of insanity himself, the devil, could send my way. The master deceiver continued to shower me with his fiery darts of dread and mistrust throughout the night, but I stood on these words from God: "God has not given us a spirit of fear, but of power and of love and of a sound mind" (2 Timothy 1:7). I gave a big sigh of relief as the message finally traveled from my head to my heart.

"The best time to go fishing is when you can get away."

ROBERT TRAVER

We waited four or five days for the report to come back. When the doctor finally called with the good news that everything was fine, Mary looked at me and said, "I knew that. I was expecting a good report." We both praised and thanked God for His Word and the power of prayer.

Mary underwent 32 days of radiation and was put on medication for five years. She keeps up her annual mammograms, and for 18 years she has remained whole and healed—cancer free.

REFLECTION

Mary Lindner

I lost my sister to breast cancer in 1994, but I never thought it would happen to me.

When my annual mammogram detected a lump that needed further testing, things moved forward very quickly. Just moments before being wheeled into the surgery, the doctor asked me in private, "If it's cancerous, would you rather have a lumpectomy or a mastectomy?"

Following the operation and coming out of the anesthesia, I was still a bit hazy, but the doctor told me that it was indeed breast cancer—stage one—and he felt he had gotten all of it.

Once I was alone in my hospital bed, I glanced over at my tray, where I had my Bible and a book brimming with healing Scriptures. Anger exploded within me, and I pounded my fist on the tray, shouting, "God, You said I would be fine, and now this report of cancer is here."

I was livid.

Shortly after that, the doctor came in and said we were awaiting the results on two more tests. They were very important because they would show whether the cancer had spread into the blood and 12 lymph nodes.

To which I immediately responded, "Oh! One for each disciple!"

Several days after that we got the good report—the blood and lymph-node test results showed no evidence of cancer in them.

Al and I stood on the faith-building words of Mark 11:22-26 and Proverbs 3:1-3. I now carry those verses in a locket Al gave me. I believed that what God said was mine, really truly was mine.

As I prayed to have that mountain of cancer removed from my body, the Lord was faithful to answer my prayer. Get to know His Word and His promises for you, and once you do, never let them go. Always expect a good report!

There is more to this story that will have to wait for another book. I continue to be an advocate of breast cancer awareness, encouraging women about the importance of annual mammograms.

Not that I am implying that I was in any personal want, for I have learned how to be content (satisfied to the point where I am not disturbed or disquieted) in whatever state I am.

PHILIPPIANS 4:11 AMP

Chapter Eleven

When Things Go South

AL LINDNER

I HAD THE INVITATION IN MY HAND, AND man, it felt good. Glancing out my window at the thick blanket of snow and the cold gray light of a Minnesota winter, the thought of fishing for big bass in 70-plus degrees in Florida seemed like a dream. I love ice fishing, but I was ready to pitch the winter gear for some fun in the sun.

The letter was from the Bass Pro Shops, inviting me to fish the upcoming Legends tournament in early February 2001. The event was to be held on the Disney lakes in

Orlando. I'd seen several fishing shows televised on these private waters in the past, and if half the stories I'd heard about the size and number of bass in these lakes were true, this tournament was for me. I'd been invited to the tournament in previous years, but because of other commitments, I had never been able to make it.

Mary and I decided to drive down early so I could enjoy some fishing with Ron. He and Dolores spend their winters in Florida on the Saint Lucie River and are only a few hours from Orlando. First we fished a few days on the river for snook and tarpon, and then we spent three days on the Stick Marsh fishing bass with shiners, which I'd done very little of. We absolutely slaughtered the bass—*big* bass—and I discovered that shiners are the only way to go when you want to catch lots of Florida-strain largemouth bass early in the season. They say shiners produce at a five-to-one ratio over artificials at that time of year—*wow*!

The morning I headed for the tournament and the rules meeting, I was as confident and as fired-up as I could be. I love the competitive side of fishing, and I fish tournaments because I believe I can win. I know the importance of confidence in winning, and I always take that into

any tournament I fish. Besides, I had been so busy putting together our television series, I hadn't fished a tournament for a long time and was looking forward to seeing old friends and competing on the water with them again before a national audience.

Participation in the tournament is by invitation only, and the list of competitors read like a who's who of tournament bass fishing—Rick Clunn, Kevin VanDam, Jay Yelas, Mark Davis, David Fritts, Jimmy Houston, and Gary Klein just to name a few. Then there were the other greats—such legends as Tom Mann, Johnny Morris, Billy Westmoreland, and others who have made a major impact on sport fishing.

We had one day of practice, and I needed that to get a good look at the unfamiliar waters. Most of the fishermen knew these waters like the back of their hand, but I had never fished a tournament on this system before. In practice I caught about 25 bass, and the biggest was about three and a half pounds. At the evening banquet, we drew amateur fishing partners as well as our takeoff numbers, and I was the second boat out. Wow—it didn't get much better than that! I was certain where I was going to open and that I'd get a quick limit.

"Man can learn a lot from fishing—when the fish are biting, no problem in the world is big enough to be remembered."

O.A. BATTISTA

What followed through the next two days was absolutely the worst performance of my entire competitive fishing career. It got so bad, I started to talk to myself. Everything I tried didn't work, and I could not put a decent fish in the boat to save my life. Meanwhile, other guys were rolling in big fish all around me. For some reason I could not get it together. By the end of the first day, I was out of the running. I had no chance of even coming close to a decent finish.

But my partner, an amateur, was doing well. On the second day he was in the hunt to win the fully rigged Tracker boat and trailer—the first-place prize for the guest amateur angler. Determined to help guide him to score big-time (and hoping to save face by at least putting him on the winning bag of fish), I followed a weed line that drops from 10 to 16 feet on a small point. We were both cranking Risto Raps, but then my partner switched to a rod with a white jig and craw and made a cast away from the break line I was following. Out of the corner of my eye I saw the bait hit the water, and *bang!*—a four and a half pounder hit. This fish added nicely to my partner's weight.

I moved the boat out to where he caught the fish, a 16-foot flat with fish suspended over nothing—no structure, no cover…just chasing bait. It wasn't long before I heard my partner set the hook again, and it was a big bass. This fish could possibly help him actually win the boat! I grabbed for the net just as the fish broke water, and I could see that it was only lightly skin hooked. The wind was blowing hard at a bad angle, and the bass was breaking water and shaking its head and could come off any second. As I reached out as far as I could, the fish turned oddly, catching the hook on the net. It momentarily wobbled precariously on the rim and then simply flipped back into the water. We both watched in stunned amazement as the fish swam away—along with my partner's new Tracker boat and trailer.

The next morning I packed up the boat and headed for home. The three-day drive from Orlando to Minnesota gave me a lot of time to think about what had just happened. Only one angler in that tournament finished lower than I did. As a competitor who loves to win, I was totally disheartened with my performance and kept asking myself what I could have done differently. Well, I never figured that out.

But as I drove across the country, I realized that I am amazingly blessed. I live in this great nation of ours. I am free to pursue my dreams and make a fine living doing what I love—fishing! I support myself through a lifestyle, not a job. And I had just fished with some of the best fishermen in the world on legendary waters with beautiful facilities and every convenience.

Can anyone who gets to do what I do ever complain that they had a bad day fishing?

One of the primary reasons God was not pleased with the children of Israel during their exodus was their murmuring and complaining. A good reminder.

REFLECTION

Mary Lindner

Neither Al nor I will ever forget this tournament. It truly changed Al's life. I should know, having listened to him mumbling to himself for hundreds of miles on our drive home from Florida. The peace of God that eventually came over him was like the calm and serenity of a quiet river as the wind dies down. Contentment is not a life free from trouble or challenges. But when the peace of God comes to rule in our hearts, and when the joy of the Lord becomes our strength, the sense of divine blessing overflows in us! Then we can say with David, "Why, my soul, are you downcast? Why so disturbed within me? Put your hope in God, for I will yet praise him, my Savior and my God" (Psalm 42:5 NIV).

*He will command his angels concerning
you to guard you in all of your ways;
they will lift you up in their hands.*

PSALM 91:11-12 NIV

Chapter Twelve

Angel on the Ice

AL LINDNER

AS I WRITE THIS, IT'S BEEN 32 YEARS SINCE I committed my life to Jesus. I was 37 in June 1982, and one of those statistically rare people who come to faith later in life. Not long after that season of spiritual transformation, I had another experience that changed my life—actually, it saved me.

In the late afternoon on the day before Thanksgiving, I decided to leave the office early and go home and catch some bluegills for our evening meal. At that time, I lived on a small lake just out of town, and it was good for panfish and bass. In our area of northern Minnesota, the small lakes usually have enough ice to walk out on safely (three to four inches) by late November. Our lake had a good three inches with no snow cover—just a solid sheet of clear ice.

When I got home, I grabbed my bucket of fishing gear, tossed in some wax worms for bait, and picked up my ice chisel. A point of land separated the bay we lived on from another small bay, which was where I usually went for bluegills, crappies, and occasional bass. That bay was only about a block away from my shoreline.

I strolled to my favorite spot and broke a hole through the ice with my chisel. It didn't take long before I started catching fish and having a great time. Both my sons were playing with some of their buddies on the ice, slipping and sliding around me. After a while they got cold and tired out and headed back to the house, leaving me alone on the ice with my thoughts.

Something is magical about the twilight hours on a lake at this time of year. The flickering sunshine reflects off the ice all around and falls softly into the hushed seclusion of the lake. I love the long, slanting bars of light that strike the treetops around the edge of the water and the deep shadows on the hills. The trees, though stripped and bare except for a few brown leaves, stand tall and strong to face the cool, bracing air of early winter.

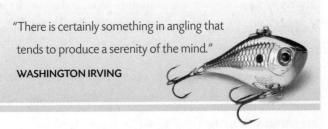

"There is certainly something in angling that tends to produce a serenity of the mind."

WASHINGTON IRVING

I enjoyed the scenery until just before dark. The bluegill bite was about over, and I had plenty of fish to fry. So I tossed my gear into the bucket along with the frozen fish, carried my ice chisel in my right hand, and headed back around the point for home. There was a scent of coming snow in the air, and I was drinking in long, deep breaths of it as I plodded along.

I got to a spot in the bay in front of my house where I know there's a little drop-off in about eight feet of water, and I suddenly stopped. I had just taken a step forward with my right foot in front, and I paused for a moment with my legs spread in this position and looked down at the ice. Silence surrounded me.

Something about the ice looked strange…something was different in a way that I'll never be able to describe. So I took my chisel from my right hand, laid it out in front of my right foot, and tapped down to check the ice. In that moment the chisel broke through the ice, and I slipped forward.

With the extra weight that went out on my right foot, the ice suddenly cracked without warning. I fell through, plunging forward into the freezing water. Instinctively, I lifted my right arm up because I saw what looked like another piece of ice. It was almost like a hole in the ice. My right arm caught at the elbow on the other end of the ice, and instantly my full weight jerked my right shoulder back really hard. The

back of my shoulder pushed all the way out—I thought I'd just dislocated my shoulder—and then…everything…went blank.

I remember nothing of what happened next. Nothing. The lights went out, outer silence became inner silence, and I sensed nothing.

The next thing I remember is kneeling on the ice at the edge of the hole, soaking wet. My left hand was supporting my weight on the ice, and my right arm was dangling loose. I could still feel my shoulder out of its socket. I stood up, knowing I was hurt bad. I leaned forward with my right shoulder and felt it pop sickeningly back into the socket.

I took a deep breath and gazed around, searching the ice for the person who pulled me out of the water. No one was on the ice but me, yet I knew I could not have possibly pulled myself out.

Fortunately, the night was not bitterly cold. I grabbed my bucket of gear and fish, trudged back up to the house, and went into the garage. I told Mary what had happened and then got out of my wet clothes. We had a nice fish dinner, but my shoulder was really starting to ache. I didn't know how bad I was injured until I laid down in bed. The pain

then became excruciating, and I had no choice but to have Mary drive me to the hospital emergency room. The medical team immobilized my arm and gave me some painkillers (which I took in abundance). In time, praise God, it healed.

Perhaps you believe there's a natural explanation for how I made it home that night, but I can tell you that if an angel hadn't been walking beside me on the lake, I would have been a goner. Angels are said to be "ministering spirits sent to serve those who will inherit salvation" (Hebrews 1:14 NIV), and my angel earned his wings that night. I just wish I could have gotten a peek, even for a second.

> So Peter was kept in prison, but the church was earnestly praying to God for him.
>
> The night before Herod was to bring him to trial, Peter was sleeping between two soldiers, bound with two chains, and sentries stood guard at the entrance. Suddenly an angel of the Lord appeared and a light shone in the cell. He struck Peter on the side and woke him up. "Quick, get up!" he said, and the chains fell off Peter's wrists.
>
> Then the angel said to him, "Put on your clothes and sandals." And Peter did so. "Wrap

your cloak around you and follow me," the angel told him. Peter followed him out of the prison, but he had no idea that what the angel was doing was really happening; he thought he was seeing a vision. They passed the first and second guards and came to the iron gate leading to the city. It opened for them by itself, and they went through it. When they had walked the length of the street, suddenly the angel left him.

Then Peter came to himself and said, "Now I know without a doubt that the Lord sent his angel and rescued me from Herod's clutches and from everything the Jewish people were hoping would happen" (Acts 12:5-11 NIV).

REFLECTION

Al Lindner

I can't tell you how many times over the past 30 years I have thought about this incident. I'll never forget that fraction of a second when the Holy Spirit warned me something was wrong, the catching of my elbow, the searing pain, and then waking from unconsciousness. I believe with all my heart that an angel of God caught me up and set me down on the edge of the ice. The Word of God is filled with stories of angelic intervention, and the psalmist said the Lord "will command his angels concerning you to guard you in all of your ways; they will lift you up in their hands" (Psalm 91:11-12 NIV). I've been in those hands at least once, and it's a great place to be.

Follow Me, and I will make you fishers of men.

MATTHEW 4:19

Chapter Thirteen

Camp Fish and the Fishers of Men

RON LINDNER

OF ALL THE VARIOUS BUSINESS VENTURES that Al, Mary, Dolores, and I put our hands to over the years, perhaps the most special one was also the most frustrating for me personally.

In 1984, after considerable prayer and godly counsel, we felt certain of God's blessing to purchase a summer camp for kids. It was situated on three small, beautifully wooded lakes just south of Leech Lake near Walker, Minnesota. The previous owners of Camp Fish had built a facility—an angling laboratory and a fishing education complex—but after four years they had not been able to make their dream financially viable.

The camp had developed a curriculum that espoused a complete outdoor way of life, instructing kids on how to fish at a very high level and acquainting them with the fishing tackle industry and the basics of aquatic biology. Al and I and some of our In-Fisherman staff volunteered our time as guest speakers and teachers and advisers. For many of the campers (approximately 700 a year), fishing became not just a pastime or a hobby or even a sport, but a *passion*! A number of them are working in the sport-fishing industry today.

By this time, the In-Fisherman Communications Network had grown beyond our magazine to include a syndicated television and radio show as well as "on the water" schools, several books, instructional videos, and traveling seminars. Our mission statement read, "Teaching North America to catch fish is our business," and we meant it. With that vision and commitment, Camp Fish seemed to fit like a glove. The story of the work we accomplished with young people there delights my heart. And the facility also served another purpose—an even higher purpose.

Kids' activities dominated the summer, but for ten years,

after Labor Day we ran an outreach at the camp that became known as the Fishers of Men Retreats. Early autumn in the North Country brings some of the best fishing opportunities of the year, and here we had a facility that not only could house and feed 100 people but also had large halls and classrooms for lectures and meetings. We also had all the equipment to produce a first-class angling experience. And our permanent staff who ran the camp were all Christians.

Prior to buying the camp, I had been meeting with a special group of recovering alcoholics who wanted to go beyond mere lip service to the 12 steps. (You'll read about my experience with AA in chapter 15.) At the time, the group was focusing on the third step—"We made a decision to turn our will and our lives over to the care of God"—and I knew from personal experience that commitment better be to Jesus Christ.

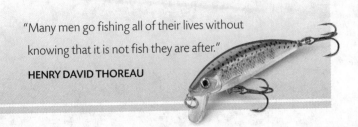

"Many men go fishing all of their lives without knowing that it is not fish they are after."

HENRY DAVID THOREAU

I thought the best way to facilitate this would be to get a group together and fly into a remote Canadian fishing camp. We would spend three intensive days of fishing and soul searching with absolutely no distractions—no televisions, radios, phones—and no way out.

So for this first effort, 13 fishermen who were born again invited 13 fishermen who were searching for the truth. Each Christian was asked to pray for his guest for the entire week preceding this retreat. Everyone attended a morning session by our evangelist, and then searchers were paired with believers to go out in the boats—but not with the person who brought them. The focus was to allow the Holy Spirit to work and speak through our lives while enjoying days of great fishing.

After dinner there was another hour or so of explaining the simple gospel, focusing only on God's biblical plan for salvation. Then we broke into small groups, and questions were encouraged. Many hours of good discussions took place in the solitude around a bonfire and under a beautiful starlit sky.

The last session before everyone flew out, the evangelist asked those who wanted to turn their life and will over to Jesus to stand up. On that first retreat, everyone did, and many made verbal confessions for Jesus. For the attendees as well as for Al and me and our Christian friends who had come along to speak and give counsel, it lived up to its billing as the "fishing trip of a lifetime"—both for fish and *for men*! (By the way, one guy caught a 13-pound walleye!)

This trip was the model for many Fishers of Men fishing trips to follow. Most of these retreats were held at Camp Fish, which hosted as many as 100 fishermen. We also tried to keep a balance of one believer to one searcher for the truth. People of various religious and nonreligious backgrounds were always welcome, and we trusted completely in the leading of the Holy Spirit to change lives. We invited evangelists to be our primary speakers, and other people (usually fishing personalities) told their faith stories. Pastors of various churches also helped out.

The method of inviting people was unique. Al and I sent invitations to Christian brothers who were avid fisherman, and they in turn sought out acquaintances and friends who had been on their hearts and who might be open to coming.

Consequently, we had folks come from all walks of life—from lawyers to farmers to accountants to salesmen to fishing guides—and from different parts of the country. All slept dormitory style, with wood-burning stoves, bunk beds, sleeping bags, and excessive snoring. The thousands of men who attended loved it.

The spiritual agenda for the retreat was always made clear, but part of the lure was the fishing. Many men came to the camp just for a chance to fish or talk with Al and the many other well-known anglers who were on hand to help. Famous bass-fishing tournament anglers, such as Shaw Grigsby and Jay Yelas, were guest speakers at one retreat. For those whose preference was walleyes, tourney champs Daryl Christensen and Mark Dorn came to give their testimonies and answer questions after sessions. For football fans, Wally Hilgenberg (16-year NFL veteran and avid fisherman) was enlisted as a speaker.

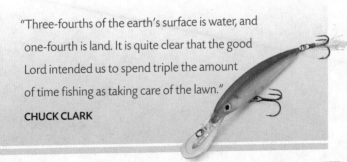

"Three-fourths of the earth's surface is water, and one-fourth is land. It is quite clear that the good Lord intended us to spend triple the amount of time fishing as taking care of the lawn."

CHUCK CLARK

Countless stories could be told of what happened at these retreats, but one story stands out in particular. An angler who was fishing Leech Lake for the weekend stopped at Camp Fish to get some information just as a session was starting in the main hall. He thought it was a fishing seminar, so he sat down and listened for a while, and then he continued on his way. He returned later that night and accepted Jesus into his life. This man has gone on to share the gospel with many others while fishing in a boat, reminiscent of the apostles who worked on the Sea of Galilee. His wife also came to faith through him, and in later years both were healed through prayer—one from cancer and the other from congestive heart failure.

The Bible states that "neither the one who plants nor the one who waters is anything, but only God, who makes things grow" (1 Corinthians 3:7 NIV), and we saw this

demonstrated over and over at the camp. We watched as individuals whose loved ones had prayed for them for years finally surrendered to Jesus Christ. Others who had walked away from faith in Christ for a time returned to Him at our retreats. Some left the camp without making a decision but later contacted us to say thanks for their special weekend and to tell us they had since become Christians. We never did an actual follow-up, but we know that a high percentage of the men came to faith. And many believers said the weekends strengthened their walk with Christ and motivated them to make positive changes in their lives.

Today, God continues to work through men who came to Christ at the camp. One is building churches in Russia. Another is a senior member of a large national Christian youth ministry. An optometrist who accepted Jesus replicated the retreats in Wisconsin. A chiropractor is doing the same in Ontario, Canada.

We know that many men were reconciled with their families and are active Christians today, bringing other family members and friends into the kingdom of God. And as an extra-special gift from the Lord to me, one of my sons came to accept Jesus at one of those retreats.

Considering all the wonderful blessings of Camp Fish and the Fishers of Men Retreats, why was I frustrated with this venture? "Every good tree bears good fruit" (Matthew 7:17), and this tree obviously bore good fruit. What was my problem?

During the decade we ran Camp Fish, it never came close to breaking even financially. Despite our love for the camp, nothing we did or tried brought it out of the deep red. We held special events for women, underprivileged kids, and troubled youth. We had father-and-sons events and parent-and-child events. We also started a newsletter called *In-Fisher Kids* and promoted the camp on television and radio through all our media outlets. We even appealed to the tackle and boating industries to help out. After ten years, however, in order for Camp Fish to function at the high level for which it was originally designed, we realized the only way was for us to subsidize it perpetually. The overhead, insurance, taxes, and short season were simply too much.

But our board of directors and financial advisers told us the In-Fisherman pockets were simply not deep enough to bear the ongoing costs. In 1994, to our dismay, we had no choice but to close Camp Fish and sell the grounds.

REFLECTION

Ron Lindner

After we sold the camp, we continued to conduct periodic Fishers of Men Retreats in different locales. And in conjunction with large tackle firms, the extensive fishing curriculum and materials we developed for teaching were donated to the US Fish and Wildlife Service and used at sites across the country to instruct kids. Parts of these are still in use today.

For me, however, it's still a puzzle. I keep thinking we may have missed God's leading somewhere. Al, Mary, and Dolores feel that God simply wanted us to have the camp for a decade, touch the lives we did, and then move on. I hope that's true. We ran the camp as long as we possibly could, trying to be good stewards of what God had given us. But closing the camp was the biggest disappointment in my In-Fisherman career. I've never been back to the grounds since we decided to sell them. I just haven't had the heart.

We recently learned that the property was acquired with plans underway to care for wounded veterans. We praise God for that.

King Solomon said, "There is a time for everything, and a season for every activity under the heavens" (Ecclesiastes 3:1 NIV). Maybe that was what Camp Fish was—a season. Evangelists and pastors who participated in events at the camp have echoed this sentiment.

Let the redeemed of the Lord say so.

PSALM 107:2

Chapter Fourteen

Let the Redeemed
of the Lord Say So

AL LINDNER

OVER THE YEARS, VARIOUS PARTIES EXPRESSED
interest in buying the In-Fisherman Communication Network. Some even made realistic proposals. However, only
when we received an offer in 1998 to sell our company to
a very large New York–based publishing firm did we begin
to seriously entertain the idea. It was a huge, life-changing
decision. After careful thought, much prayer, and 24 wonderful years, Ron, Dolores, Mary, and I knew it was time to
sell. A deal was struck, and I agreed to stay on for three years
under a work contract and a non-compete agreement.

Ron, on the other hand, decided to weigh other options.

Not being the retirement type, he immediately set up an office and once again called on his family as personnel. Keeping his finger on the pulse of the sport-fishing industry, Ron busied himself writing articles for various national magazines. And ever inventive, he also began tinkering with new tackle concepts and developed the No-Snagg Slip Sinker, which in 2000 became a runaway bestseller for Lindy Tackle.

I knew I had to get out of the way and let the new owners of In-Fish spread their wings and develop their vision. Their conglomerate included hunting, fishing, and other publications, some in the automotive world. They also bought a number of other prominent fishing magazines, such as *Fly Fisherman* and *Florida Sportsman*, and were expanding into the burgeoning Internet world.

I also wanted to spend some quality time with my son Troy, who was honing his skills and beginning to make a name for himself in the Southwestern bass circuits. So I signed on only to do the television shows and would continue for the balance of my contract, which would end in May 2002.

Meanwhile, behind the scenes, God was working in diverse situations and preparing each of our hearts for what was to come next. Isaiah 43:19 sums it up: "I am about to do something new…Do you not see it? I will make a pathway through the wilderness" (NLT).

In April of 2000, Ron was visiting a small bait shop in southern Florida and inadvertently bumped into Tom Makin and Mark Fisher, officers of Rapala, the world's largest manufacturer of fishing lures and related products. In the parking lot, after some small talk and updating, Ron learned that Rapala was interested in creating a three-hour, three-part DVD series that encompassed the company's long and storied history. The series would feature freshwater and saltwater species, it would include product demonstrations, and it would be peppered with instructional "how to" segments by their legendary pro staff.

Coincidently (or actually, by God's design), a few years earlier my nephew Bill Lindner (Ron's oldest son), an acclaimed outdoor photographer, had done some work for Rapala that featured the historical aspects of the company. It included reenactments of the early days of founder Lauri Rapala and other compelling footage. Bill had this film footage and other outtakes in his archives at his studio in Saint Paul, Minnesota.

When Ron mentioned this potential project to his sons James, Dan, and Bill, he lit a fire of enthusiasm. It dovetailed perfectly with their own visions and future ambitions.

What happened next is legendary in the Lindner family lore.

James, Dan, and Bill soon met with Rapala and reached an agreement in principal to produce the DVD series. This is hard to comprehend today, but the deal was sealed with a handshake and based purely on trust. As I understand it, no formal contract was ever written.

Dan and James left their posts at In-Fish and joined forces with Bill, whose own creative know-how and vast library of historical footage gave them a great jump-start. Using Ron's offices as a base of operations, they installed

editing suites, moved in three of Bill's fish tanks for studio underwater photography, and purchased video cameras and other equipment. As they combined their talents and imaginative ideas, all rockets were boosting full blast.

Ron's "chance" conversation at the bait shop parking lot in southern Florida had become the launching pad for the Lindner Media Productions company.

That first enterprise was a huge undertaking and took a little more than a year to complete. It included saltwater and freshwater footage from the Gulf of Mexico to the Arctic. The completed DVD project has segments of historic and underwater footage that appear in thousands of places on the Internet—with cuts played countless times on YouTube and websites the world over.

With their first project nearing completion and my work contract coming to an end, change was in the air. One morning in early February, while running on the treadmill (as I do almost every day when I'm home), I began to ask, "What do you have next for me, Lord?"

I clearly sensed a response in my heart. "I want you to get back into television, but this time I want you to reference My Word and the things I have done in your life."

I could see it—a brief spiritual and inspirational closing of some kind at the end of every fishing show, planting seeds in the hearts of those who love to fish but would never tune in to a religious program.

After sharing this with Mary, she suggested we fly to Florida to talk with Ron and Dolores, who were enjoying their annual respite from winter, soaking up rays with family, and chasing tarpon and snook. Mary and I hopped on a flight, and that evening I shared with them what God had laid on my heart and what I envisioned. Immediately the four of us had peace in our hearts and were in complete agreement with going back on television and honoring God at the same time.

"Let the redeemed of the Lord say so." That is exactly what we set out to do.

We were off and running, excited about the new thing God was doing. All we needed were some sponsors and the networks to air on. For this, we needed some expertise, and no one was better for the job than my longtime friend and sidekick Dan Sura. He was consulting at the time, and we prevailed upon him to consult for us.

The day after the non-compete agreement was up—

May 8, 2002—Dan and I went on the road. By the end of the month we had verbal agreements for all 12 sponsor categories. In a couple more months we had all the contracts finalized, payments made, and network and station details ironed out. In June we began filming our inaugural series. That was a late date to start the filming season, but we were blessed with unseasonably great weather and cooperative fish. For the first time, all our new shows would close with a short, inspirational message.

As a testimony to God's faithfulness, in 2015 we will celebrate our forty-fifth consecutive year on television. Thank You, Lord Jesus.

Al Lindner

Including a spiritual message in our show on secular television stations and networks was a huge endeavor, and we had no idea how it would be received. In 2003 the spiritual climate was not what it is in 2015. A lot has changed in the past decade or so—and not always for the better. Yet I am happy to report that the response of the viewing public to the ending of our show has been overwhelmingly positive through the years.

We occasionally receive a negative reply, and it generally goes something like this: "We really like the fishing portion of your program, but can you cut the biblical baloney at the end?"

I personally answer every response, and my answer usually goes something like this: "I fought in Vietnam to maintain your freedom to write me a letter and express your opinion. But I also fought so I would be free to express mine. If you like the fishing portion of our show, please continue to watch. But if you don't like the end, simply shut it off. That is what freedom of speech is all about."

Jesus said, "Whoever confesses Me before men, him I will also confess before My Father who is in heaven" (Matthew 10:32). That's an offer no one should pass up.

Creating a new television series brings many new challenges. We are constantly refining our methodology to get the most dramatic underwater shots. We are flying drones to capture amazing aerial imagery. To stay on the cutting edge, we are constantly dealing with new technology. Ron and I recently chuckled while sitting in one of our editing suites—when we started out four and a half decades ago, we used hand-cranked film cameras, and we edited footage on a Moviola with hand-cranked rewinds.

So when we say we've come a long way, baby, we aren't kidding. Lindner Media has grown into a full-service creative production company with deep roots in the outdoors. Our talented multimedia specialists produce original outdoor television programming, national television commercials, point-of-purchase video displays, video catalogs, and on-screen presentations for sales meetings and corporate training sessions. We also produce and host our own nationally syndicated television series, *Lindner's Angling Edge*.

I'm thankful for the Lord's promise that "with God all things are possible" (Matthew 19:26).

The wages of sin is death, but the gift of God is eternal life in Christ Jesus our Lord.

ROMANS 6:23

Chapter Fifteen

The End of the Line

RON LINDNER

MY LOVE FOR FISHING BEGAN WHEN I WAS A young child vacationing at my parents' lake cabin in northern Wisconsin. It was a great escape from our big-city life in Chicago, and everything about the sport fascinated me. In fact as kids, Al and I even started a little company out of our parents' basement in Chicago, selling lures under the name Lindner Manufacturing Company—complete with our parents' address on the lure boxes!

Even during a stint in the army and then 12 years of working on road-construction crews in Chicago, my only dream was to move my family out of the city to where lakes abound. I constantly thought about new lures, new reels, new lakes, and new techniques for catching fish. Al and I spent our weeknights making lures in my basement, tested them on weekend fishing trips, and read everything we could find on fishing. I remember telling Dolores that if I could make $10,000 a year and work in the sport-fishing industry, I would be the happiest man in the world!

In 1965, during Al's tour of duty in Vietnam, he and I decided to follow our dreams, move "up north," and find our way into the sport-fishing business. When he returned in 1966, we moved first to Wisconsin and then to Minnesota, where we started making tackle again and began a fishing-guide business as well. Over the next 13 years, Al and I invented and marketed numerous lures, some selling in the millions. We launched and later sold the Lindy Tackle Company, started the In-Fisherman Media Network, authored many books and articles, fished tournaments, produced radio shows, published a fishing magazine, and aired a nationally syndicated television show.

Despite our success, real and lasting happiness eluded me. Something was missing in my life, but I didn't know what it was. During this time, I lived my fantasy of fishing from the Atlantic to the Pacific and from the Arctic to the Caribbean while my wife was home raising our seven children without me. I ran with some hard-living people, which caught up with me when I got my third DUI in 1973. My drinking problem forced me to join Alcoholics Anonymous.

For the next five years I struggled with alcohol. I'd stay clean for months, but then a night or two of drinking was followed by weeks of guilt, remorse, and depression. I sincerely did not want to drink, but the temptation was unrelenting. And the longer I stayed sober, the more intense the pressure seemed.

The breaking point came on Good Friday in 1978. After nine months of sobriety, I was driving to the Northwest Sportshow in Minneapolis, and deep down I knew I was going to drink that weekend. Despite my training in AA, I walked into the show and went straight to the beer stand. I inhaled the first beer and then another…and more throughout the day. After the show closed, I went to a restaurant bar with some folks and downed several Manhattans before a dark black curtain rolled over my consciousness…and it was lights-out.

I came to in my hotel room with crumpled, dirty clothes spread around the floor. My head was swimming, I was pouring sweat, and my arm and shoulder were black and blue. About $8 in change was on the nightstand, although I remember having $200 in cash. After taking a quick shower, I headed down to the lobby and asked if I had any messages. The clerk asked if I'd like to check out, but I told him I'd be staying until Sunday. He gave me an odd look and said it was Sunday. I had not only blacked out but also lost an entire day and a half!

When I went to the hotel parking lot, my car was missing. In a panic, I reported it stolen, only to have the police find it parked two blocks away where I had obviously left it. Later, I learned that I had made a complete fool of myself at the Sportshow and in the restaurant.

Loaded with shame and utter emptiness, I started the three-hour drive back home. Flipping through radio

stations, I stopped as a preacher quoted from 1 Corinthians 6:9-10: "Do you not know that wrongdoers will not inherit the kingdom of God? Do not be deceived: Neither the sexually immoral nor idolators nor adulterers nor men who have sex with men nor thieves nor the greedy nor *drunkards...*"

That hit me like a ton of bricks. I was a drunk—a lost, damaged soul. Although I had always believed there was a God, nothing in my life reflected it. I was out of excuses about turning the corner on a better tomorrow. Tomorrow was now here.

When I arrived home, I didn't tell Dolores what had happened. But before long she said, "An evangelist is preaching over in Crosby-Ironton tomorrow, and I'd like to hear him. Do you want to go?"

"Sure," I mumbled, feeling so guilty I would have agreed to anything.

The next evening we went to the little town of Crosby. The evangelist's name was Lowell Lundstrom, and little by little, his words began to meld with the words of the radio preacher. Pointedly, his message came with the conviction of the Holy Spirit that drunkards would never see the kingdom of heaven. I suddenly realized that unless God had an alternate plan, I was at the end of the line.

Then I heard Lundstrom say something about forgiveness and a new life and becoming a new creature. I wasn't sure what all this meant, but I instinctively knew it was good news that I desperately needed! When he asked if anyone wanted to come forward and receive Jesus, I jumped out of my seat and almost ran to the stage! I didn't care if anyone joined me—I wasn't even quite sure what was happening. Soft music was playing, and a few others slowly filtered up. To my left an old man was weeping.

Suddenly I felt a hand grab my arm. I looked over and saw Dolores smiling at me. My heart melted on the spot.

I don't know how close I had come to spooling God's reel, but I knew I was close! All the fight was out of me. As Lundstrom led us in prayer, we confessed our sins, asked God to forgive us, and invited Jesus Christ to come into our lives as Lord and Savior.

Years would pass before I fully realized what God did for me at that moment. But the most obvious and incredible change was a complete freedom from alcoholism! With the gentle net of His grace, He had scooped me into His boat. And this was not catch and release. He put me into His live well of eternal life—forever!

Ron Lindner

Looking back on my life, the biggest snag to my finding true happiness was my complete misunderstanding of God's love and grace. Only after years of abusive drinking and a blackout weekend in Minneapolis did I begin to understand that salvation is a free gift of God that comes to us by faith. We can never earn or merit it. We simply need to believe the truth that Jesus Christ gave His life and blood to forgive us of our sins. It's that easy!

Perhaps you have run out of tomorrows and dragged yourself out to the end of the line. If you want to find peace with God, remember, "If you declare with your mouth, 'Jesus is Lord,' and believe in your heart that God raised him from the dead, you will be saved" (Romans 10:9 NIV).

If you will receive Jesus Christ into your life today, He will come in and change you in ways you never imagined.

After receiving Jesus at the Crosby meeting, later that night I sat alone in our living room, reading and rereading the little booklet Lowell gave me called *Saved for Sure*. Over and over in my mind I was pondering, *Is it really this simple?* As my eye glanced out the picture window overlooking the lake at two thirty in the morning, I saw the northern lights explode into the night sky like never before or since. A colossal celestial celebration welcomed me into God's kingdom.

Jesus answered, "Very truly I tell you, no one can enter the kingdom of God unless they are born of water and the Spirit...You should not be surprised at my saying, 'You must be born again.'"

JOHN 3:5,7 NIV

Chapter Sixteen

One Last Cast

RON LINDNER

AL AND I HAVE LIVED MOST OF OUR LIVES doing what we love to do, and fishing has never grown old. When it's first light on the water, we want to be there, and at the end of the day, it's still hard to take that last cast. I'd like a nickel for every cast I've made after saying, "Just one more."

Before we close this book, however, we'd like to take one last cast in your direction. You've read our stories, and you've seen some of the ways our faith has influenced the decisions we've had to make along life's long road. It's possible that you're not certain what Al and I mean when we say we're born-again Christians.

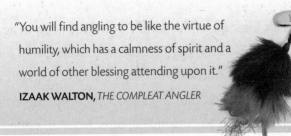

I realize the term "born-again Christian" has developed some negative connotations over the years. Today, some say the term is redundant—if you call yourself a Christian, you must be born again, and nothing else is necessary. Others point to the negative, unloving actions of some who call themselves "born again," and they conclude that the words are meaningless. For many people, the term has been so misused that it has become just another tired, religious cliché

For most of our lives, Al and I were no different from most people regarding all things spiritual. It isn't that we didn't believe in God—faith just didn't seem to make that much difference in our lives. Spiritual words, such as "born again," had little meaning—negatively or positively. We simply didn't understand. But as you've read, that all changed for both of us, and the "new birth" transformed our lives and our families.

When Jesus spoke the words "You must be born again" to Nicodemus in the third chapter of the Gospel of John, He gave a direct, uncompromising statement. Jesus did not offer those words as simply a good idea, a nice suggestion, or something Nicodemus might consider as an option or alternative to something else. As a Pharisee, Nicodemus was already a deeply religious man. As a member of the Sanhedrin, the supreme council of the Jews, he was a national leader. Nicodemus certainly didn't need to become more religious—he was already stuffed to the gills with religion. Jesus said that to enter the kingdom of God, one must first have his or her heart changed. Nicodemus (and I) struggled to understand this.

You've read my personal account of how God intervened in my life after a drunken blackout weekend in Minneapolis. When I heard the words Jesus spoke to Nicodemus, "You must be born again," I did not understand how God could do that in my life. But I was at the end of my line, and I finally understood that I must do things His way to find peace, serenity, and joy. Only later, after I surrendered my life and will to the care of Jesus Christ as my personal Savior, did I begin to fully understand the meaning of being born again.

Since that time, I've heard many phrases used to describe the process of salvation—"making Jesus Lord of your life," "accepting Jesus as your personal Savior," "coming to the cross," "making a decision for Christ," "having a personal relationship with Jesus," "confessing Christ as Lord"...and the list goes on and on. Still, the process of being born again, regardless of what it's called, comes down to this: We acknowledge we are sinners, we repent (turn away from our sin), we accept that only through Jesus's death on the cross can we be forgiven and have our sins washed away, and we ask Jesus to come into our hearts through the Holy Spirit and make us new people.

If you're at the end of the line in your life or moved to seek peace for your soul, you can pray a simple prayer I learned many years ago.

> Father, I'm a sinner, and I'm sorry for the sins in my life. I ask You to forgive me and to cleanse my heart with the blood of Your Son Jesus. I give You my life. Jesus, come into my heart as Lord and Savior, and direct my paths by the Holy Spirit from this day forward. Thank You for giving Your life for me, and help me to always live for You. Amen.

This is certainly not the end of the matter. In fact, it's only the beginning of a personal relationship with God. Where will it lead? Well, ultimately into the eternal kingdom of God, just as Jesus told Nicodemus it would. But I guarantee that in the meantime, along the way, wherever God leads, you will experience the most exciting, exhilarating, and satisfying portion of your entire life.

REFLECTION

Al Lindner

Wherever Jesus Christ went, it was reported that "the blind receive sight, the lame walk, those who have leprosy are cleansed, the deaf hear, the dead are raised, and the good news is proclaimed to the poor" (Matthew 11:5 NIV). The blind opened their eyes for the first time and saw their God. The ears of the deaf were healed, and the first sound they heard was the voice of Jesus Christ. The lame man sprang up from the dust and walked and leapt and praised God—and was judged a fool by those who had never known such joy. Those who had never spoken suddenly broke a lifetime of silence with songs of praise.

When the grace of God came into Ron's life and into my heart and made us new men, it removed the spiritual blindness, deafness, and brokenness of our lives.

It was an impossible task for anyone but God. But amazing grace had its way with us, and today there is no condemnation for those who are in Christ Jesus. We can say in truth, "Old things have passed away... all things have become new," and "We are more than conquerors through Him who loved us" (2 Corinthians 5:17; Romans 8:37).

Today there are many new philosophies, new revelations, and new ways of trying to please God (or "gods"). I see people chasing after them to try to seize this or that promise, only to return hungrier and thirstier than ever. Don't go that way. True faith in Jesus will deliver you from any emptiness. Grace will flow into your heart, and delivering mercy will be the anchor of your life.

When Christ is in your heart, real life is possible, joy is possible, and peace is possible—in all circumstances and all places. Everything your redeemed soul can desire, it possesses in Christ. Endless "rivers of life" flow in and through those who have Jesus in their hearts.

About the Authors

With long careers spanning the most revolutionary years in sport-fishing history, Al and Ron Lindner have become renowned industry leaders.

They are cofounders of Lindy Tackle as well as the In-Fisherman Communications Network, both of which have since been sold. With its numerous radio and television programs and magazines, In-Fisherman became North America's largest multispecies fishing network.

In 2002, Ron and Al, along with Ron's sons James and Daniel, launched Lindner Media Productions. Ron and Al's talented multimedia specialists have produced original outdoor television programming, national television commercials, point-of-purchase video displays, video catalogs, and on-screen presentations for sales meetings and corporate training sessions. They also produce and host their own nationally syndicated television series, *Lindner's Angling Edge*.

Together Ron and Al have developed a comprehensive lake, river, and reservoir identification classification system, a fish response calendar, and the famed $F + L + P = S$ formula (fish plus location plus presentation equals success), which has been described as the algebra of angling.

Al is hailed as one of the world's best all-around anglers. He still spends 200 days a year on the water. Al was first inducted into and later enshrined in the National Freshwater Fishing Hall of Fame. He also has been inducted into five other fishing Halls of Fame. Besides being one of the earliest participants in professional major bass tournaments in the South and a two-time Bassmaster tournament winner and qualifying for numerous classic events, he has also won major walleye and bass tournaments in the North.

With more than fifty awards at last count, Al's long work with teaching youth to fish reached a high point when the US Fish and Wildlife Service used his In-FisherKIDS Camp Fish formula as a nationwide teaching tool. Of all his titles, he prefers that of angling educator, a work he tirelessly pursues.

Ron was inducted into the National Freshwater Fishing Hall of Fame for his contribution and dedication to the sport of freshwater angling and its conservation and history. In pursuing his dream he has worn many hats—professional guide, tackle and equipment designer, inventor (with three patents and thirty unique designs to his credit), tackle manufacturer, professional tournament angler, promoter, writer, publisher, television producer, and radio host. His work in angling theory includes the coauthorship of 15 books, the writing of countless published magazine articles, and the production of thousands of radio and television scripts.

Throughout their professional lives, the Lindner brothers blended their work with raising families and growing in their evangelical faith. Ron and his wife, Dolores, have seven children (four sons and three daughters). Al and his wife, Mary, have two sons. Every member of both families has worked in some aspect of the sport-fishing industry. Ron and Al believe that involving the family turns a job or a career into a shared lifestyle.

Most importantly, Al and Ron Lindner remain incessantly curious fishermen and consummate innovators. So after all these years, for them, there's still nothing that beats a good day's fishing!

The Next Generation

Estelle and Art Lindner,
Al and Ron's parents

TOP LEFT: The Millennium Men—Ray Scott, Johnny Morris, and Al, *In-Fisherman*, 2000
TOP RIGHT: Ron's daughter, Dawn Lindner, and granddaughter, Elizabeth, *Catch* magazine, 2003
BOTTOM LEFT: Ron reading to Al at the cabin on Grindstone Lake, Wisconsin
BOTTOM RIGHT: Al with the first fish caught off Ron's dock on Gull Lake, Minnesota

Great is the LORD and most worthy of praise;
  his greatness no one can fathom.
One generation commends your works to another;
  they will tell of your mighty acts.
They speak of the glorious splendor of your majesty—
  and I will meditate on your wonderful works.
They will tell of the power of your awesome works—
  and I will proclaim your great deeds.
They will celebrate your abundant goodness
  and joyfully sing of your righteousness.

PSALM 145:3-7 NIV

Al & Ron's grandmother,
"BUSHA" Anna Belz at
lake cabin

CLOCKWISE FROM LEFT: Al's son Troy Lindner, *Outdoor Life*, May 2002
Ron and Al, *North American Fisherman*, 2003
Ron and Nick Lindner (James's son)
Ron's son Daniel Lindner, *Saltwater Sportsman*, September 1999
Ron, Al, and James Lindner, Basswest USA

Photography by Ron's son Bill Lindner

CONTACT INFORMATION

Find out more about Lindner Media Productions at
www.lindnermedia.com
or write us at
**Lindner Media Productions
7393 Clearwater Road
Baxter, MN 56425
(218-829-9500)**

Follow Lindner's Angling Edge at
**www.anglingedge.com
www.facebook.com/LindnersAnglingEdge**

You'll also find us on YouTube, GodTube, and Roku.

To learn more about Harvest House books and
to read sample chapters, visit our website:

www.harvesthousepublishers.com

HARVEST HOUSE PUBLISHERS
EUGENE, OREGON